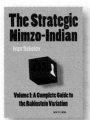

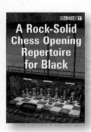

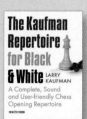

2012 Issue 3

NEW IN CHESS

PUBLISHER: **Allard Hoogland** EDITORS-IN-CHIEF: **Dirk Jan ten Geuzendam, Jan Timman**

6 NIC's Café

10 The Mozart of Chess
Adam Feinstein pays a compelling tribute to José Raúl Capablanca, the Cuban genius, who believed that chess had been invented for him.

24 Problems in Plovdiv
At the European Individual Championship the zero-tolerance rule and a new anti-draw measure caused a lot of commotion and frustration.

32 Interview
Dmitry Jakovenko, the new European Champion, talks to Vladimir Barsky about his passion for mathematics and his ambitions in chess.

44 Saturday Night Fever
Nigel Short weighs the horrors and merits of weekenders.

46 Chess City Reykjavik
Dirk Jan ten Geuzendam returned to Iceland for the Reykjavik Open, an increasingly popular destination for pros and amateurs from all corners of the earth. Top-seed Fabiano Caruana came and delivered.

10 The Mozart of Chess

24 Plovdiv

76 Valentina Gunina

92 Jan Timman

'At school everything was monotonous: the subjects, the lessons, the rules: boring daily life... I liked being different somehow. A chess player has a completely different life! But, true, it's very hard – the constant travelling, dragging an unwieldy suitcase on the metro...' – Valentina Gunina

Just Checking 98

COLOPHON p.9
SUBSCRIPTIONS p.96

Reykjavik 46

Dmitry Jakovenko 32

Bobby Fischer Comes Home 66

Through the Luking Glass 88

THE CHESS MYSTERIES OF SHERLOCK HOLMES

66 Bobby Fischer Comes Home
Helgi Olafsson wrote a book about his complex and memorable friendship with Bobby Fischer during the American's last years in Iceland.

72 Beware, TN!!
Hans Ree was guided through memory lane as he read an overview of 40 years of theoretical novelties in Chess Informant.

76 The Adrenaline Lover
European Women's Champion Valentina Gunina talks about the sacrifices she and her family had to make and the adrenaline that makes it all worth it.

88 Through the Luking Glass
Luke McShane enjoyed two books crammed with 'remarkably clear explanations'.

92 Baden-Baden again
Jan Timman takes a look at the decisive clash in the German Bundesliga.

98 Just Checking
Which three people would Gawain Jones like to invite for dinner?

CONTRIBUTORS TO THIS ISSUE
Vladimir Barsky, Dejan Bojkov, Fabiano Caruana, Adam Feinstein, Laurent Fressinet, Valentina Gunina, Charles Hertan, Dmitry Jakovenko, Gawain Jones, Vladimir Malakhov, Luke McShane, Helgi Olafsson, Hans Ree, Nigel Short, Jan Timman, Hou Yifan

PHOTOS AND ILLUSTRATIONS
Vladimir Barsky, David DeLucia Collection, Einar Einarsson, Hrafn Jökulsson, Pall G. Jonsson, Anastasiya Karlovich, Elena Klimets, John Saunders

COVER PHOTO
Jose Raul Capablanca: Daniel DeMol Collection

Was it worth it?

What is the value of a chess game? In our materialistic times, one would be inclined to say that a game's value is determined by the difference it makes in prize-money. But what if it were a game played by a great champion of the past in a private setting, and never seen by anyone?

Twenty-five years ago, in New In Chess 1987/4, we published a letter by Olga Capablanca Clark, the widow of the Cuban World Champion, which had been forwarded to us by chess historian Edward Winter. In the letter, Mrs Capablanca Clark offered an unknown game of her late husband for sale and raised every collector's curiosity with an unforgettable sales pitch. The game had been played in Paris, probably in 1938, in Hotel Regina, quite near the Louvre. She had one of her 'frequent bad colds' and while she stayed in bed to recuperate, their good friend Savielly Tartakower paid

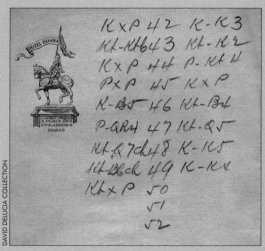

Capablanca's handwriting remained clear and steady till the last moves.

them a visit. At one point, Tartakower took out a chess set and much to her surprise Capablanca agreed to play a game. 'Of course he won', and then he took the hotel stationary on which he had written down the moves and gave it to her as a present, saying: 'Take it and hide it well. Some day in years to

come it will buy you a beautiful bijou.'

Apparently, that moment had come and 'in view of the exceptional nature of the game and the surrounding circumstances, no offer under ten thousand U.S. dollars will be accepted'.

That reserve was not met and in 1994 Olga Capablanca Clark died,

Olga and José Raúl Capablanca, a glamorous couple.

leaving Capa fans to wonder where the 'score-sheet' was and how beautiful the game had really been. Both questions have now been answered by the publication of *In Memoriam*, the stunning two-volume set in which David DeLucia presents the highlights of his amazing chess collection. Amid revealing letters, signed photos and a wealth of other Capablanca 'ephemera', the sheets on which the mysterious game was written down are shown. Publishing the game is a generous deed, as the game score must have lost much of its value now that the myth no longer exists. In the first 30 or so moves, nothing much happens and then Capa efficiently exploits a couple of endgame inaccuracies by his opponent.

VO 18.3 – A50
José Raúl Capablanca
Savielly Tartakower
Paris 1938(?)

1.d4 ♘f6 2.c4 b6 3.♘c3 ♗b7 4.f3 d5 5.cxd5 ♘xd5 6.e4 ♘xc3 7.bxc3 e6 8.♗e3 ♘d7 9.♗c4 ♗d6 10.♘e2 0-0 11.0-0 c5 12.e5 cxd4 13.cxd4 ♗e7 14.f4 g6 15.♘g3 ♕h8 16.♕d3 ♖g8 17.♖fd1 ♖c8 18.♖ac1 ♗b8 19.d5

♗xd5 20.♗xd5 ♕xd5 21.♕xd5 exd5 22.♖xc8 ♖xc8 23.♖xd5 ♖d8 24.♖xd8+ ♗xd8 25.♔f2 ♘c6 26.♔f3 f5 27.♘e2 ♔g7 28.g4 fxg4+ 29.♔xg4 ♔f7 30.♔f3 ♗e6 31.♔e4 b5 32.♘c3 a6 33.♗c5 ♗e7 34.♗b6

34...♗d7 Defending against the knight coming to d5 with 34...♘b4 and keeping the king on e6 was better. **35.♘d5 a5 36.♘c3 b4 37.♘a4 ♗d8** If he stops the king from penetrating with 37...♔e6, it's hard to see how White can win. **38.♗xd8 ♔xd8 39.♔d5 ♘a7 40.♔c5**

Now White picks up the pawns and wins easily. **40...♔d7 41.♔b6 ♘c8+ 42.♔xa5 ♔e6 43.♘b6 ♘e7 44.♔xb4 g5 45.fxg5 ♔xe5 46.♔c5 ♘f5 47.a4 ♘d4 48.♘d7+ ♔e4 49.♘f6+ ♔e5 50.♘xh7** Black resigned.

New dates, please

Immediately after his company Agon had come to an agreement with FIDE to organize the World Championship Cycle, General Director Andrew Paulson travelled to meet all the parties affected by his original plan to have the Candidates' tournament in London this autumn. After lengthy talks in various countries Paulson saw no other way out than to move the Candidates' to March 2013. They still will be held in London and, as was an-

Agon's Andrew Paulson saw no other option than to move the Candidates' to March 2013.

nounced later, will be sponsored by the state-owned oil company SOCAR from Azerbaijan. Paulson's diplomatic solution was welcomed by the players and organizers involved. In Bilbao a sigh of relief was heaved that they will not run the risk of losing players in the Grand Slam Final because of the proximity of the Candidates', and Malcolm Pein, organizer of the London Chess Classic, needed little time to confirm that from December 1-10, the fourth edition of Classic will take place anyway.

Around the same time, the organizers of the traditional Ciudad de Linares tournament issued a press release that offered no reasons for cheering. For the second year running they were forced to cancel their event. They denied that financial problems played a role, but finding proper dates had been impossible. Hopefully they will try to make a comeback next year, although it seems to be a bad omen that their traditional 'slot' at the end of February and beginning of March is no longer an option.

WhereChess

The new dates of the Candidates' tournament were confirmed at the second quarter FIDE Presidential Board meeting in Elista. Everyone present was in a good mood, as besides the meeting the 50th birthday of Kirsan Ilyumzhinov was celebrated. The small square in Chess City was named after the FIDE president and he was (finally) awarded the title of Hero of Kalmykia.

On their way to Elista, the FIDE board passed through Moscow where, at the invitation of Ilyumzhinov, they attended a chess evening in the House of Writers, the historic building where Soviet writer and Nobel Prize laureate Boris Pasternak was once expelled from the Writers' Union. Among the other guests were the first (and last) President of the USSR Mikhail Gorbachev, the Russian president's aide Arkady Dvorkovich, famous conductor Vladimir Spivakov, film director

Mikhail Gorbachov at the chess night in the House of Writers. On the right his granddaughter Ksenia.

Stanislav Govorukhin and legendary ice-hockey goalkeeper Vladislav Tretiak. By way of entertainment, European champion Dmitry Jakovenko and Alexander Grischuk played a blitz match (2½-2½) and Vlad Tkachiev won all his five games in a blindfold simul, including the one against Ilyumzhinov.

It was the first 'public' appearance of Tkachiev since the mysterious disappearance of the website WhyChess that he and his brother Evgeny enthusiastically launched not that long ago. First the site was no longer updated and then it vanished completely. Apparently, the sponsor, whom Tkachiev described in these pages as 'someone who loves chess and is not in competition with FIDE', no longer supplied money. When no more money was arriving, the Tkachiev brothers lost interest too and heeded the legendary

**Vlad Tkachiev:
'WhyBlindfoldChess? WhyNot!'**

credo of Rustam Kamsky: 'Organizer pay, Gata play!' Or the other way round, of course.

Pow Whack Zap Ding Liren

Ding Liren is rapidly becoming the most famous Chinese chess player that no one knows. The 19-year-old grandmaster, born in Wenzhou, in the province of Zhejiang, has hardly played any tournaments of importance outside his country, but that didn't stop him from claiming the national title for the third(!) time at the Chinese championships in Xingua. The first time Ding Liren won the title was in 2009, when at the age of 16 he became the youngest champion

Ding Liren: three-time Chinese Champion.

ever. This time he finished a full point ahead of a field that included experienced GMs such as Wang Yue, Bu Xiangzhi and Ni Hao. This is what he did to Lu Shanglei.

QO 16.9 – D24
**Ding Liren
Lu Shanglei**
Xinghua 2012

1.♘f3 ♘f6 2.c4 e6 3.d4 d5 4.♘c3 dxc4 5.e4 ♗b4 6.♗xc4 A popular pawn sacrifice. **6...♘xe4 7.0-0 ♘xc3** After 7...♘f6 8.♕a4+ ♘c6 9.♗g5 ♗e7 10.♗xf6 ♗xf6 11.d5 Black got into trouble in Aronian-Anand, Bilbao 2011. **8.bxc3 ♗e7** Taking a second pawn with 8...♗xc3 leaves Black with an unenviable position after 9.♖b1, but a decent alternative is 8...♗d6. **9.♘e5 0-0 10.♕g4 c5?** Safer is 10...♘c6. **11.♗h6 ♗f6 12.♗d3!** And all this for only one pawn. **12...♖e8 13.f4!**

Strong and concrete play! **13...g6**

This runs into a forceful sacrifice, but what else? After 13...cxd4 14.♗xh7+! ♔xh7 15.♗xg7! ♔xg7 (or 15...♔g8 16.♕h5+ ♔xg7 17.♕xf7+ ♔h6 18.♖f3) 16.♕h5+ ♔g8 17.♕xf7+ ♔h8 18.♖f3 wins. And after 13...♘c6 14.♖f3! is too strong, e.g. 14...g6 (14...cxd4 15.♖g3) 15.♗xg6 fxg6 16.♘xg6 e5 17.f5. **14.♗xg6! fxg6 15.♘xg6 hxg6 16.♕xg6+ ♔h8 17.♗g5!**

17...♗xg5 Also hopeless is 17...♖f8 18.♖f3 ♗xg5 19.♖h3+ ♗h4 20.♕h5+. **18.fxg5! ♖e7 19.♕h6+ ♔g8 20.g6! ♘d7 21.♖f3 ♘f8 22.♖af1 ♘xg6 23.♖g3 ♖g7 24.♖xg6** Black resigned. ∎

COLOPHON

PUBLISHER: Allard Hoogland
EDITORS-IN-CHIEF:
Dirk Jan ten Geuzendam, Jan Timman
EDITORS: Peter Boel, René Olthof
ART-DIRECTION: Jan Scholtus
PRODUCTION: Joop de Groot
TRANSLATORS:
Sarah Hurst, Ken Neat, Piet Verhagen
SALES AND ADVERTISING: Casper Pieters

© No part of this magazine may be reproduced, stored in a retrieval system or transmitted in any form or by any means, recording or otherwise, without the prior permission of the publisher.

**NEW IN CHESS
P.O. BOX 1093
1810 KB ALKMAAR
THE NETHERLANDS**

PHONE: 00-31-(0)72-51 27 137
FAX: 00-31-(0)72-51 58 234
E-MAIL:
SUBSCRIPTIONS: nic@newinchess.com
EDITORS: editors@newinchess.com
SALES AND ADVERTISING:
casper.pieters@newinchess.com

BANK DETAILS:
IBAN: NL41ABNA 0589126024
BIC: ABNANL2A in favour of Interchess BV, Alkmaar, The Netherlands

WWW.NEWINCHESS.COM

A comparison with Wolfgang Amadeus Mozart may well be the highest praise a chess player can earn. In an interview in *New In Chess* in 1992, Miguel Najdorf suggested José Raúl Capablanca, Bobby Fischer and Garry Kasparov as the main candidates for the enviable sobriquet. In recent years, Lubos Kavalek's description in the *Washington Post* of Magnus Carlsen as the Mozart of chess has been echoed in hundreds of articles about the Norwegian phenomenon. **Adam Feinstein** has no doubts. Seventy years after Capa's death he agrees with Don Miguel's first choice and expresses his admiration and fascination with a compelling tribute to the Cuban genius, who believed that chess had been invented for him.

Young Capablanca and his father at the chess board. His father was an educated man and like many Cuban military at the time, a keen chess player.

JOSÉ RAÚL CAPABLANCA

The Mozart of Chess

DAVID DELUCIA COLLECTION

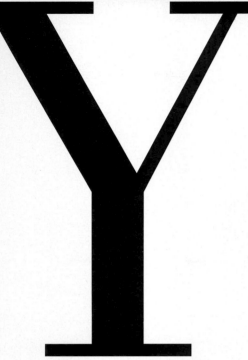

*Y*ou who come from Cuba, have you seen Capablanca?
How is Capablanca?
What was Capablanca like?
Where is Capablanca?
Capablanca is not on his throne,
But he is there, wandering,
exerting his mastery over the world

These words, by the late Nicolas Guillén, Cuba's national poet, illustrate just how profoundly the presence of Latin America's first and only world chess champion, José Raúl Capablanca – 'the Mozart of chess' – still lingers on in this Caribbean island.

Capablanca himself is, of course, long dead. He succumbed exactly seventy years ago this year, at the age of just 53, as he watched a game at his beloved Manhattan Chess Club in New York. He left a widow, Olga Chagodayeva, who outlived him by half a century, dying in 1994 at the age of 95. I met her once, in her seventh-floor apartment on New York's Park Avenue, in the mid-1980s, and she was still a very imposing and charming figure as she recalled her husband with huge affection.

Why is it so apt to compare Capablanca with Mozart? Because both men were virtuosi, masters of technique but with a seemingly magical intuition to make the difficult look easy. Capablanca's finest games have the delicious harmony of a Mozart symphony.

José Raúl Capablanca y Graupera was born in Castillo del Príncipe – a military installation in Havana – on November 19, 1888. He was the second child of an officer in the Spanish Army, José María Capablanca Fernández and María Graupera Marín. Capablanca's original nationality was Spanish, since Cuba still belonged to Spain and would do so until it gained its independence ten years later.

His father was an educated man and, like many Cuban military at the time, a keen chess player. In fact, at the end of the nineteenth century, Havana was the leading centre for chess in the whole of the Americas, together with New York and New Orleans. (Cuba, incidentally, is said to be the first chess-playing nation in the Americas – there is a reference to a game played there dating back to 1518.) José Raúl grew up listening to conversations about tactics and strategy, a fact which, in his own words, probably inspired his early love for the game of chess, which he said he found even more fascinating than a story from the *Thousand and One Nights*. Most people know the legend: at the age of four, he was watching his father play and pointed out that he had made an illegal move with his knight. Astonished – maybe insulted – his father challenged his son to a game and lost. The boy was every bit as astounding a prodigy as the young Mozart.

José Raúl 's father began to take his son to the Havana Chess Club and, by the age of 11, he was already among the strongest players in Cuba. In November 1901, Capablanca took on Juan Corzo in a match for the championship of Cuba. He lost the first two games but rallied to emerge victorious by four wins to three and five draws.

He completed his studies at the Instituto de Bachillerato in Matanzas, northern Cuba. Then, thanks to financial assistance from a Cuban sugar industrialist friend of the family, Ramón San Pelayo, the 16-year-old Capablanca was shipped off to the United States to learn English at Woodycliff School in New Jersey. From there he enrolled at Colombia University in New York to study chemical engineering. It was in New York that he found women – and the Manhattan Chess Club. It was there, too, that he began to be called 'Capa.'

On the night of April 6, 1906, at the age of 18, he took part in a lightning tournament in which he defeated the World Champion, Emanuel Lasker, before going on to win the event, to the astonishment of everyone present. Shaking his hand, Lasker declared: 'It's extraordinary – you didn't make any mistakes.' (By his own admission, Lasker was a little disconcerted by the attention soon being showered on the newcomer. He recalled visiting a school in his native Germany and, as the pupils started to recite the Greek alphabet, he could not help giving a start when the children reached the letter 'kappa.')

Inevitably, Ramón San Pelayo soon heard about Capablanca's chess exploits, rather than his studies. He threatened to withdraw his financing – unimpressed by either Capablanca's good grades at Colombia in 1906-1907 or the young man's pledge to specialise in sugar engineering once he graduated. Many years later, Capablanca's university roommate, Bernard Epstein, wrote to Capa's widow, Olga, to say that Capa had sold some of his clothes to fund his continued stay in the U.S., as well as offering articles to the press. He was even reported to have played for a professional U.S. baseball team for a while. What is clear is that Capablanca was far too proud a young man to ask Pelayo to reconsider his withdrawal of financing. And Capa certainly refused to drop his passion for chess. Thanks to his friend Herman Helms – the publisher of the *American Chess Bulletin* – he placed an advertisement

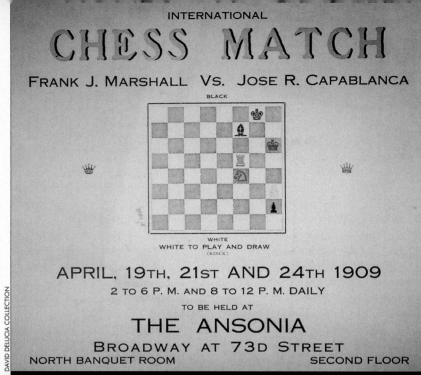

INTERNATIONAL
CHESS MATCH
FRANK J. MARSHALL VS. JOSE R. CAPABLANCA

BLACK

WHITE
WHITE TO PLAY AND DRAW
(RINCK)

APRIL, 19TH, 21ST AND 24TH 1909
2 TO 6 P. M. AND 8 TO 12 P. M. DAILY
TO BE HELD AT
THE ANSONIA
BROADWAY AT 73D STREET
NORTH BANQUET ROOM   SECOND FLOOR

In 1909 Capablanca sensationally beat Marshall 8-1, draws not counting. Marshall said his worst move had been to wake Capablanca up.

A photo of the proud and confident winner of San Sebastián 1911 from the tournament book.

offering simultaneous chess displays. The response was astonishing and by 1908, Capa found himself criss-crossing the United States by train. Out of 734 games, he won 703, drew 19 and lost just 12.

In 1909, Capablanca defeated the great Frank Marshall in a friendly match. Marshall recalled later that the young man – just 21 – seemed bored and even nodded off at the chessboard on more than one occasion. Marshall said his worst move had been to wake Capablanca up. But the American generously forgave the young Cuban upstart and with the help of Arístides Martínez, the then president of the Manhattan Chess Club, he arranged for him to be invited to the legendary San Sebastián tournament in northern Spain in 1911. Capablanca headed for Europe for the first time on board the ill-fated *Lusitania* (the ship would be sunk by a German torpedo in May 1915).

Before arriving in Spain, he stopped off in London, where he was interviewed by *The Evening News*. His supreme confidence – which some critics soon took for arrogance – was already plainly in evidence: 'I learnt to play chess before reading, but I have

never studied,' he told his interviewer.

The San Sebastián event boasted the strongest field yet assembled – all the greatest players on the planet were taking part, apart from the World Champion, Lasker. At the start of the event, Aaron Nimzowitsch and Osip Bernstein objected to the presence of the young man because he had not yet won a major tournament. Sensationally, however, Capablanca won this one – a feat which sent ripples around the chess world.

That same year, 1911, Capablanca felt ready to challenge Lasker for the world title. The German accepted but stipulated 17 conditions. There followed an unpleasant exchange of letters between the two men. Capablanca accused Lasker of being dishonest, while the German urged Capa to adopt a more modest approach because he was behaving as if he were the champion and Lasker were the challenger. Capablanca rejected Lasker's conditions and the match did not take place. An interesting recent discovery was a letter written by Capablanca to a close friend, Rolando Illa – eight-times Argentinian chess champion – dated January 26, 1912,

in which he claimed that Lasker was suffering from '*mieditis*' [a Spanish neologism of Capablanca's implying a medical condition consisting of fear of playing him].

The relationship between the two men deteriorated rapidly. Years later, however, in his book *My Chess Career* (published in 1920), Capablanca offered a candid assessment of what would have happened if he had played Lasker in 1911. He said he firmly believed Lasker would have won the match 'with relative ease' due to his greater experience – adding that, for this reason, the German had committed a huge blunder by not agreeing to the title contest then and there. Capa acknowledged that, in 1911, he had much to learn about the openings, the middlegame and about how to defend difficult positions.

In 1912, Capablanca returned briefly to Cuba before leaving for Argentina and Uruguay, where he gave further simultaneous displays. The following year he played in two tournaments in New York. He won both – one with the perfect score of 13 wins out of 13. Back in Cuba, at the Havana tournament of 1913, he reportedly lost seven kilos in weight but only one game –

JOSÉ RAÚL CAPABLANCA

against Frank Marshall, from a winning position – and obtained second place overall. (Reuben Fine claimed that Capa asked the Mayor of Havana to clear the hall of all spectators so that they could not witness his resignation against Marshall, although Edward Winter has insisted that Fine's story has no foundation whatsoever in fact and that the 600 or so spectators, mostly American, understandably gave their compatriot Marshall a standing ovation. Marshall himself corroborated this latter version of events.)

In 1913, the Cuban Foreign Ministry appointed Capablanca as an ambassador-at-large – a welcome sinecure. By now, he was already the most famous Cuban on the planet. The following year he crossed the Atlantic again to play at the famous tournament in St Petersburg, Russia, and there he made friends with the Soviet composer Sergey Prokofiev. In the tournament he came second, drawing with the eventual tournament winner, Lasker. At the closing gala, the two men were reconciled after their three years of animosity. It was during this 1914 tournament, nevertheless, that Capablanca came to an agreement with most of the world top players for future title contests, to avoid the difficulties he was having in finalising his match with Lasker. According to these new rules, the champion would put his title at stake once a year, but only if the challenger could come up with a purse of at least one thousand dollars. (The 'London Rules' of 1922 increased the minimum purse to 10,000 dollars. Of this sum, the champion would receive 2,000 dollars in advance and the rest would be divided up after the match: 60 per cent for the winner, 40 per cent for the loser.)

Capa found himself directly caught up in the First World War. His German boat, the *Cap Vilanex*, was due to sail across the Atlantic from Hamburg, when war broke out in July 1914 and the ship was forced to pull into Lisbon – Portugal remained neutral in the conflict. Another ship, the

Amazon, resumed the journey to the United States two days later.

He spent the whole of the duration of the war in New York, while chess tournaments were interrupted. Once, in 1918, two members of the U.S. counter-espionage service paid him a visit and wanted to check up on his foreign correspondence. They were mystified by a sheet of paper bearing the oddest symbols which must have seemed like a coded message. Capa told them, in all seriousness, that they concerned a liberation plan. He then showed them over a chessboard how he intended to free his position. The 'coded message' was the score of a game.

The identity card of José Raúl Capablanca, commercial attaché at the Cuban legation in Brussels, issued on July 17, 1935.

Before leaving for Europe to take part in the celebrated Hastings tournament in Britain in 1919, Capablanca once again demonstrated his supreme self-confidence when he told *The New York Times* that he knew more about chess than any other contemporary master and that he could play simultaneously against the thirty best players in the United States without losing a single game.

Capablanca backed up these words

by crushing the field at Hastings, scoring an almost unbelievable 10½ points out of 11. He was lionised in the UK. Brian Harley, in his book *Chess and Its Stars*, depicted the crowds thronging to Hastings to stare at their dashing idol – said to be as handsome as Rudolph Valentino – with an adoring gaze. On December 2, 1919, he gave a simultaneous display in the House of Commons in London against 38 Members of Parliament and he was unofficially named World Champion – although Capa himself insisted that the title would come only after he had won it fairly and squarely against Lasker. He had certainly cemented his right to be the challenger: between 1915 and 1919, he had won 43 games, made 10 draws and suffered a single defeat – against the Austrian-American, Oscar Chajes, at the Rice Memorial Tournament in New York in 1916.

Yet despite the worldwide adulation, and his role with the Cuban diplomatic service, Capablanca was not a rich man. He gave a fascinating interview to the Cuban magazine, *Bohe-*

mia, in 1920, in which he declared: 'You have to dress the part, and you know how much that costs today? In London I paid four pounds for a dozen roses, which I presented to a distinguished lady, the wife of a well-known English gentleman in whose luxurious car I was being driven around... A quarter-of-an-hour ride in a taxi cab costs five or six pesos. Hotels, trains, boats, tips, clothes, shoes, theatre tickets, return invitations to people who have been attentive to me. You can imagine what all that costs. With what the Cuban state pays me and with what I can earn when tournaments offer prizes, add-

DAVID DELUCIA COLLECTION

Capablanca versus Oscar Chajes at a tournament in 1918 in the Manhattan Chess Club. Behind him Frank Marshall is playing Dawid Janowski.

ing it all up and keeping my outlay ridiculously low, I don't even have anything left to pay the valets' tips.'

On January 2, 1920, Capablanca sat down with Lasker for lunch in a restaurant in The Hague and began thrashing out some of the conditions for their world title contest. By January 23, an official communiqué announced that the match was on, at an as yet undisclosed date and place. Some manic media speculation ensued, variously naming the venue as Rio de Janeiro, Buenos Aires, New York, Chicago and Holland.

At this point, the Havana Chess Club entered the fray, beginning complex negotiations for the match against Lasker in the Cuban capital. The encounter finally began on March 15, 1921, at Havana's Unión Club. In a revealing article in the Dutch newspaper, *De Telegraaf*, just before the opening game, Lasker wrote that, while he himself took Julius Caesar as his role model – because he always led his forces against those of least resistance – Capablanca's model was Ulysses, because he was 'wise, clever, strong and inventive.'

Capablanca won the Havana match by four victories to none, with ten

draws, to become the new World Champion. We would have to wait another seventy-nine years – when Vladimir Kramnik beat Garry Kasparov in 2000 – to witness the world chess crown won without losing a single game. It is true that Lasker had not grown acclimatised to the humidity of Havana, but after the second game, the venue was moved to a cooler building closer to the sea and scheduling was switched to the evening.

Lasker generously hailed the man who had stripped him of his crown. Nevertheless, in his final article for *De Telegraaf*, on April 30, 1921, Lasker made some oddly contradictory remarks. Starting off by stating that he liked Capa's style of play, he went on to criticise his own poor performance, before adding: 'I have watched chess lose the charm of adventure, I've seen how mechanical it has become, how it has been reduced to a question of memory. I deplore this unnecessarily rapid development, I haven't gone down that route, even though I can see that it has become necessary to do so, just as it is necessary for a man to die at some point (...) Capablanca seems to personify this automatic style (...) Chess, in its current state,

will suffer death by drawn games (...) They will have to establish new rules (...) Is Capablanca the ideal player, the supreme master of chess? I don't think so. But he deserves to be world champion (...) Capablanca's style is surprising for its logic (...) [His] imagination has been suppressed (...)'

The same year that Capablanca became World Champion was notable for other reasons. Capablanca married his first wife, Gloria Simoni Betancourt. She came from a well-off family in Camagüey, in central Cuba. With the purse from his victory over Lasker, Capablanca bought himself and his new bride a comfortable house in Havana, which he dubbed Villa Gloria, in what used to be called the Avenida Cuarta, now in the district of Playa. In 1923 they had a son, also called José Raúl – remembered today for being the man who moved Bobby Fischer's pieces when Fischer participated by Telex in the fourth Capablanca Memorial Tournament in Havana in 1965 – and in 1925, a daughter, Gloria.

In a very touching letter to his son, dated October 7, 1925, Capablanca urged him to be honest, to learn to

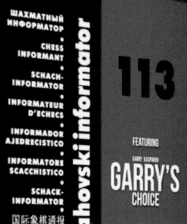
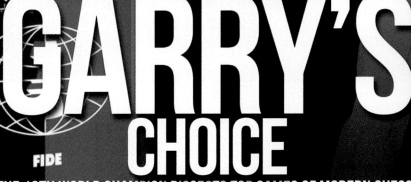

swim and box 'so that you can handle yourself at sea as well as on land', to read widely and to avoid playing cards, if possible (something Capa himself never avoided – he was a keen and very brilliant bridge-player). José Raúl junior went on to become a lawyer.

Capablanca also published another book, *Chess Fundamentals*, in 1921. One of his collaborators on the book recalled in 1944 that the set which he and Capablanca used to analyse positions was basic, to say the very least: the board was a crudely cut piece of cheap cloth, while the pieces came from different sets – except for the white rooks, which were represented by two sugar cubes!

Capa's first tournament after gaining the world crown was the London tournament in 1922. He won, ahead of the likes of Alexander Alekhine, Géza Maroczy, Richard Réti, Akiba Rubinstein, Milan Vidmar and Max Euwe.

He played no chess at all the following year, 1923, dedicating it to his family, spending time cooking soufflés for guests at their Havana home, and never setting foot in a chess club. On June 28, 1923, his father died in Havana at the age of 61 from a tumour which developed after he fell from a horse. In sorrow, Capa went into reclusion for a few more months.

By 1924 Capablanca had achieved a feat that remains unequalled to this day: he had lost just one game in eight years. That defeat was against Richard Réti in the 1924 New York tournament where he had been suffering from influenza. The man some considered a 'chess machine' had shown himself to be human, after all – but he still finished in second place in that tournament, ahead of Alekhine.

As the late Cuban author Guillermo Cabrera Infante noted, Bobby Fischer, with all his eccentricities, was the Howard Hughes of chess – playing the game as if it represented a constant campaign to annihilate the personality of the opponent – whereas Capa-

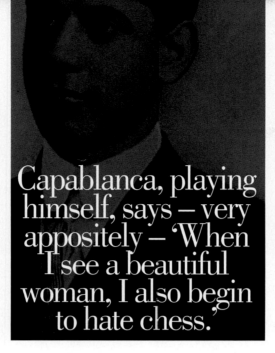

Capablanca, playing himself, says – very appositely – 'When I see a beautiful woman, I also begin to hate chess.'

blanca represented 'supreme self-confidence and the absolute conviction that the game was his: chess had been invented for him.'

And yet, Capa seemed only half interested in chess. The female form was apparently what most vividly captured his imagination. During the 1922 London tournament he was invited, along with Alekhine – with whom he was still on friendly terms – to see the famous Bluebell Girls performing. Throughout the evening Alekhine's eyes were directed at a position on his pocket chess set, while Capa's gaze was focused firmly on the girls' legs!

Shortly after the increasingly Right-wing and authoritarian President Gerardo Machado took power in Cuba on May 20, 1925, Capa received an invitation to participate in the Moscow tournament that year. Many friends advised him that a visit to the new Socialist state would harm his career. The Cuban Justice Minister, José María Barraqué, officially advised Capa to reject Moscow's invitation. Capa ignored this and other appeals and set off for Europe.

He arrived in Moscow to a hero's welcome. The World Champion was in town. The shops were full of chess merchandise. Capablanca became a film star. The great Russian film director Vsevolod Pudovkin shot his

18-minute short film, *Chess Fever*, in which Capablanca, playing himself, says – very appositely – 'When I see a beautiful woman, I also begin to hate chess.' While in Moscow, Capablanca – an avid reader – made close friendships with Soviet writers, poets and artists – not to mention famous ballerinas. Female admirers would queue up to present him with boxes of chocolates. His presence was welcomed in the USSR as breaking down the cultural blockade of the recently formed Socialist state.

In the Moscow tournament itself, however, Capa could come only third, behind Bogoljubow and Lasker. Chess lovers suddenly dared to wonder whether the champion – although still only 37 – was already in decline. They also pointed to his defeat in a simultaneous display he gave in Leningrad during the Moscow tournament. The 14-year-old boy who beat him on this occasion was a certain Mikhail Botvinnik – who would go on to become World Champion 23 years later.

There was reputed to have been an important visitor to a simultaneous display Capablanca gave at the Kremlin during his stay in Moscow – Joseph Stalin was watching behind a curtain, or at least that is what Capa's widow, Olga, claimed he had told her. After the closing ceremony, Capablanca was reportedly escorted to Stalin's office, where the two men drank tea together and spoke about Russia's civil war. If this meeting did actually take place, one can only speculate what the Cuban – who had been a guest of honour of the Tsars in the St Petersburg tournament in 1914 – found to say about this war.

Before leaving the Russian capital Capa gave a very interesting interview in which he appeared to refute Lasker's assessment of his 'calculating' play four years earlier. The Cuban made this bold, and surprising appeal: 'Let's get rid of the mechanical, let's abandon scientific theories and let's seek out a new battle of ideas.' He was revealing a romanticism which

Join the world's biggest chess server. At playchess.com you will meet 20,000 chess lovers every day, from all over the world. You will immediately be able to find an opponent of your own playing strength, or if you fancy watching, you can kibitz grandmaster games and follow world class tournaments. Indulge in the best of playchess.com now and be ready for top-class live-commentary of the coming world-ch match Anand-Gelfand!

7 reasons for premium membership

1. All world class tournaments with live commentary
See it live when Carlsen, Anand, Kramnik & Co are battling out in classic tournaments, candidates tournaments or the world championship itself with triumph or defeat on the line. Enjoy fascinating live analysis from the very top commentators like Daniel King, Yasser Seirawan or Maurice Ashley and experience the decisive moments in world class chess up close and personal.

2. Round-up shows – the survey of the important events of the day
When there are top tournaments, playchess commentators offer you an evening survey of the high points of the day. What was the most spectacular game? Who gave away the win or managed to save the draw with a trick? Which player has the best chances of overall victory?

3. An unbeatable team – the commentators on playchess.com
Premium members will find awaiting them on playchess.com a team of authors of the highest class. Daniel King is a real jack of all trades as far as chess is concerned: experienced grandmaster, author of numerous books, committed trainer and the most popular chess presenter of all. With his analyses Maurice Ashley provides the best of proof that chess is exciting and that it can be presented in a fascinating and entertaining way. In his career Yasser Seirawan has

already crossed swords with Kasparov, Karpov, Tal, Larsen and many other greats. On playchess.com the American's comments on what is happening are always eloquent and competent.

4. "Power Play" show with Daniel King
In the DVD series with the same name the former leading English player talks about a multitude of themes, motifs and strategies which are all worth knowing. What is required for a successful attack on the king? How do you improve the cooperation of your own pieces? etc. etc. The "Power Play" show extends your chess know-how in an extremely entertaining fashion.

5. Ask the experts – what you always wanted to know
Spectators ask, experts answer. Right from the start this new format was very popular on playchess.com. No wonder, because in the first six broadcasts questions from premium members were fielded by, for example, Peter Svidler, Rustam Kasimdzhanov, Victor Bologan and Jan Gustafsson. Grab the opportunity! Ask a genuine expert what he thinks about some idea in your favourite opening line!

6. "Endgame Magic" show with GM Karsten Müller
In his monthly show, the leading international endgame expert Dr. Karsten Müller singles out endgames from recent tournament practice and passes on entertaining insights into the constantly amazing world of the endgame.

7. Learning from the masters means masterly learning!

Playchess.com offers you a complete training programme – from traps in the opening all the way through to endgame theory. International Master Robert Ris explains the openings and shows you sharp surprise weapons.
IM Merijn van Delft puts recent grandmaster games under the microscope and tries, along with the spectators, to analyse the plans and strategies of these connoisseurs.

CHESSBASE GMBH · OSTERBEKSTR. 90a · D-22297 HAMBURG · TEL ++(49) 40/639060-12 · FAX ++(49) 40/6301282 · WWW.CHESSBASE.COM · INFO@CHESSBASE.COM
CHESSBASE DEALER: INTERCHESS B.V., P. O. Box 1093, NL-1810 KB ALKMAAR, phone (++31)72 51 27 137, fax (++31)72 51 58 234, www.newinchess.com

Lasker – and many others – had not discerned. As his Cuban biographer, Miguel Angel Sánchez, has noted, a totally scientific player would have studied the game ceaselessly, whereas Capablanca rarely opened a chess book. Except, that is, when it came to teaching Latin America's first female international chess master – the Cuban, María Teresa Mora Iturralde. (She played three games against Capablanca, all in simultaneous displays. She won two of them and drew the other.)

In 1931 Capablanca played a 10-game match against Dutch grandmaster Max Euwe in Amsterdam. Capablanca won 6-4.

The chess set used in the 1927 World Championship match in Buenos Aires, against Alekhine.

Unlike Alekhine, Capablanca had clearly been impressed by at least some of what he had seen in Bolshevik Russia. On his return to Havana, Capa was at pains to emphasise the high level of official support given to Soviet chess players. 'The [Soviet] government considers it [chess] a superior means of educating the people,' he said.

On December 7, 1926, Capablanca's mother died. Just as after his father's death, he reacted by going into reclusion and was virtually not seen in public until the New York tournament in February and March 1927 witnessed his resounding victory over his five adversaries: Alekhine (by now, a naturalised French citizen), Nimzowitsch, Vidmar, Spielmann and Marshall. The margin of victory – he was unbeaten and placed 2½ points ahead of his nearest rival, Alekhine – went some limited way to dampen the grief he felt over the loss of his mother, as did the finalisation of his world title match with Alekhine in Buenos Aires.

Capablanca was ill-prepared for this contest – as well as overconfident after his New York success. The world shared his confidence. Few gave Alekhine any hope. The Austrian grandmaster Rudolf Spielmann thought Alekhine would not win a single game. Capa arrived in Buenos Aires on September 10, 1927 and was whisked off in a limousine to the Hotel Plaza. According to one local journalist, the 39-year-old world champion had put on some weight and the first grey hairs were starting to appear on his head.

The match began with a shock – Capablanca's first ever defeat to Alekhine in the first game. A rumour ran around after this loss that Capablanca had spent the previous night with a well-known Spanish-born Argentinian film star, Gloria Guz-mán, who would later make several films with Carlos Gardel, the famous tango singer and composer. Capa was also said to have been playing cards, dominoes and billiards at night, and was even reported to have been seen placing a bet at the horse races, as well as strolling arm in arm with another Argentinian beauty down Buenos Aires' Avenida Corrientes. During the match, he missed several chances to win games and appeared uncharacteristically lacking in confidence by the end of the contest.

Capablanca resigned the final game, on November 29, 1927, conceding his world crown to Alekhine in a gracious handwritten note. The chess world gave a collective gasp of astonishment. He had lost by three victories to Alekhine's six, with 18 draws. It was the longest ever world title match – eclipsed only by the marathon 1984/85 battle between Anatoly Karpov and Garry Kasparov.

Capa made no excuses – although he did point out later that the weather had been even more suffocatingly hot in Buenos Aires than back home in Havana. But fascinatingly, he described Alekhine as 'a cold calculator, measured, mathematical. He is no lover of the imagination, which is what produces beautiful games.' This, of course, was precisely how Capa's own style was depicted and remains so to this day. Alekhine seemed to be deliberately adopting his opponent's own chess 'persona' – and the strategy worked.

The loss of the world crown to Alekhine seriously affected Capa's spirits. He stayed on in Buenos Aires for another two weeks, trying to analyse what had gone wrong while attempting to dodge the attentions of the press. On his way back to Cuba he gave further

of 10 x 10 squares, instead of sixty-four, with ten pawns on each side and two extra pieces per player. He called the two extra pieces the 'archbishop' and the 'chancellor'. The archbishop would move like a bishop and knight combined while the chancellor would move like a rook and knight combined, This would allow the archbishop to checkmate the king on its own. He compared this movement with that of billiards, at which

to abolish castling – because castling was unknown in the ancient version of chess. Ironic, because Capablanca himself was always a stickler for the importance of castling as early as possible.

Then began one of the most memorable cat-and-mouse games in the history of sport. Capablanca and Alekhine still felt huge admiration for each other's games, but they quickly came to loathe each other on a personal level. Initially, Alekhine said that he would be happy to grant Capablanca a rematch, but not before 1929 and only on the proviso that Capa conformed with the 'London Rules' which Capablanca himself had laid down after winning the world crown from Lasker in 1921. But the Cuban was unable to raise the requisite 10,000 dollars. Alekhine insisted that Capablanca remained his most serious and danger challenger. Intriguingly, Alekhine said this was because Capablanca knew how to complicate positions. How odd: Capablanca's reputation today is that of a simplifier!

Capa was nothing if not resilient. Despite the fact that the defeat to Alekhine in the 1927 match had knocked him back, he continued to achieve remarkable results in the late-1920s. He won in Berlin and Budapest in 1928, Budapest again and Hastings in 1929. At another tournament – Carlsbad in August, 1929 – at which, for the first time in history a woman, Vera Menchik, took part – Capablanca was deep in thought when he noticed a familiar face watching from the auditorium: Alexander Alekhine. Furious, Capa sent two notes to the tournament arbiters asking for the World Champion to be removed from the hall.

It seems that when Capablanca did finally manage to raise the requisite 10,000 dollars to challenge Alekhine, the incumbent then insisted that the parlous state of the world economy – after the Wall Street Crash – meant that this sum was no longer worth anything like as much as it had been and

Ramsgate 1929. Capablanca watches the game Yates-Koltanowski.

DAVID DELUCIA COLLECTION

simultaneous displays in Brazil before arriving crestfallen in Havana. On top of losing his world title, his wife, Gloria, had apparently learnt about his dalliances with other women. He spent the next eight months, it is said, trying to repair his marriage. He himself declared that he was losing his love for chess. Indeed, at the end of 1927, he told an interviewer that he had been in decline since 1917: 'The conviction in my own strength, which was a reflection of my general infallibility in judging positions, has disappeared.'

It was at around this time that Capablanca began proposing a new variant of chess, to be played on a board

he also happened to be an expert. He later moderated the proposed size of the board from 10 x 10 to 10 x 8, after playing a number of trial games with the English master Edward Lasker (who later said that these games rarely lasted longer than 30 moves).

The great Cuban poet and novelist, José Lezama Lima, in his short essay dedicated to Capablanca, called the new variant 'baroque' – and he meant it as a compliment. But the suggested changes were greeted with scorn by many fellow players, who saw them as a sign of Capa's arrogance or, even worse, his disenchantment with the beautiful game. Ironically, Emanuel Lasker countered that a better idea would be insisted that the money had to handed over in gold. Capablanca was appalled at what he perceived as a new ploy on Alekhine's part to avoid the rematch. (Instead, Alekhine chose to play two title matches against Efim Bogoljubow, winning them both comfortably.)

The next decade opened promisingly for Capa. He won in Ramsgate, Barcelona and Hastings in 1930, and New York in 1931. Meanwhile, back home in Cuba, popular protests against the Machado dictatorship – which stripped Capablanca of his Foreign Service position in 1931 – were growing by the day. Capa's elder brother Ramiro narrowly escaped being killed in a police raid. Capa hid him in his house until he was able to find asylum in the Mexican Embassy in Havana. The Justice Minister Barraqué recommended that Capablanca leave Cuba. This time he heeded Barraqué's advice and took a boat leaving for Valparaíso in Chile, stopped off in Panama and then caught a steamer to Los Angeles. He stayed in Hollywood until 1933, when he learnt that the Machado regime had fallen. On his return to Cuba, the new government appointed him Cuban commercial attaché in New York.

Capablanca took this diplomatic role seriously. In 1934 he was invited to a breakfast at the Soviet Embassy in Washington, where he met the USSR's Ambassador to the U.S., Alexander Troyanovsky. The Russian invited his guest to play a game of chess, which Capablanca won, after which Troyanovsky's wife asked how her husband had played. With the charm which so often characterised his one-to-one encounters, Capa replied: 'The Ambassador played with such ingenuity and accepted defeat with such good humour that, to tell the truth, I don't know who ended up winning!' As a result of this meeting Capablanca recommended that the Cuban government consider establishing diplomatic relations with Communist Russia, as the U.S. had done the previous year.

Capa emphasised his own friendly feelings towards the Soviet Union. These feelings remain entirely mutual. Remarkably, there have been more books written in Russia about Capablanca than about any foreign personality other than Marx, Engels, Churchill, Gramsci, Cervantes and Sigmund Freud. Among the 200 foreign personalities most easily recognised by the Russian population in 1990, Capablanca came in in 27th place.

In the spring of 1934, Capablanca met Olga Chagodayeva, either at a reception at the Cuban Consulate in New York or at a party at the home of one of Olga's friends. She claimed that he told her there and then: 'You and I are going to get married.' Olga had led an adventurous life. Born in the Caucasus in 1898, she grew up in the Georgian capital Tbilisi. After the Bolshevik Revolution she made her way to Constantinople, where she married a White Russian émigré cavalryman – Chagodayev, rumoured to be a prince descended from Genghis Khan – in 1920. When he died she inherited the title of princess. She then married an American Olympic athlete from whom she was divorced when she met Capablanca.

Olga and Capablanca did not marry immediately. Olga was free to do so, but Capa was officially still married to Gloria – hence the scandal in high circles when the couple travelled the world together for the next four years. Olga seems to have breathed new life into his chess ambitions (even though she herself would later claim that he

would rather have been a musician or a doctor). He published a new book, *A Primer of Chess*, in 1935.

He took Olga with him to the Nottingham tournament in 1936 – introducing her as his 'fiancée and future wife'. He won the tournament, ahead of the World Champion, Max Euwe (who had beaten Alekhine in 1935), Lasker, Reuben Fine, Samuel Reshevsky, Salo Flohr and Savielly Tartakower. The Nottingham tournament was notable for the first encounter between Capa and Alekhine since the 1927 débâcle. Capablanca won that personal battle and must have been delighted to see Alekhine finish the tournament down in sixth place – but would he ever win the war for a rematch? (Olga claimed to have met Alekhine during a tournament in the Czech city of Podebrady in 1936, at which Capa was not playing, and she asked her fellow Russian why he was refusing to grant Capablanca a rematch. Was it because he was afraid he might lose, she suggested – at which point, according to her version of events, Alekhine became visibly nervous and brought the conversation abruptly to an end.)

Capa wanted Olga to accompany him to Moscow later the same year but, at the last minute, the Soviet Embassy in Paris suggested that this would be an unwise move given Olga's White Russian past. Alekhine's loss of his world title to Euwe in 1935 – partly attributed to his problems with alcoholism – gave Capa renewed hope that he might regain the crown, hopes that were given a further boost when he emerged victorious at the 1936 Moscow International Tournament, ahead of Botvinnik, Lasker and others.

Capablanca was appalled at what he perceived as a new ploy on Alekhine's part to avoid the rematch.

His new-found self-confidence remained virtually watertight. Once, while sitting in a Paris café, a stranger came up to him and invited him to a game of chess. Capa immediately took his queen and put it in his pocket, offering queen odds. Offended, the stranger said: 'You don't know who I am. How can you be so sure that I won't win?' To which Capablanca replied: 'Sir, if you could beat me, I'd know who you were!'

In 1937 Euwe granted Alekhine a rematch and the Russian easily regained his crown. This dealt a new blow to Capa's chances of regaining the world title. The personal animosity deepened. The great Argentinian grandmaster Miguel Najdorf claimed that, during a conversation with Alekhine, he had wanted to stay on good terms with the Russian and so spoke in negative terms of Capablanca's play. Alekhine interrupted him firmly and said: 'You are free to speak ill of Capablanca as a person, but never about his play. In chess, he was a genius.'

After Gloria finally granted Capablanca a divorce in Havana, he and Olga were married in Elkton, Maryland, on October 20, 1938. José Raúl and Olga made a very glamorous couple – his good looks matching her blonde beauty to perfection. When I met her in the 1980s, Olga recalled how they would go to watch horse racing and how Capa loved to cook. Contrary to the general belief he was not teetotal, but he drank very moderately and did not smoke. 'He was a very refined, cultured man, interested in the arts', she told me. They would play cards together and communicated in French, because despite his love for Russia he never learnt more than a few words of the language. I did manage to ask Olga whether it was difficult to live with a man who was such a celebrated womaniser. She said she was fully aware of his reputation, but she insisted that, once they were married, she was the only woman in his life. She also pointed out that her husband was a humanitarian who had rescued many Jewish refugees from the Nazis. His brother Aquiles was the architect who designed one of Havana's main synagogues, Beth Shalom.

The very day after their wedding, the newly-weds set out for Europe, where Capablanca was to play in the AVRO tournament in the Netherlands in 1938. It was here that he and Alekhine met over the board for the final time. Capa was unwell with the high blood pressure that had begun to plague him over the previous few years. Neither man was willing to speak to the other face to face. Theirs was a double-header at AVRO. Their first game was drawn, and the second – played on November 19, Capablanca's fiftieth birthday – ended when Capablanca lost on time (in a lost position) for only the second time in his life in an official game.

In 1939, on the eve of the outbreak of the Second World War, Capablanca returned to Buenos Aires, this time for the eighth Chess Olympiad. This was a historic tournament in many ways: it was Cuba's début appearance at an Olympiad and it would be Capablanca's last tournament. As captain of the Cuban team he emerged unbeaten with seven wins and nine draws. When Cuba came up against France, he avoided playing Alekhine on top board by stepping down and putting Alberto López in his place. This must have irritated Alekhine and his mood was not lightened at the closing ceremony when Capa was given a protracted standing ovation as he received the prize for best top board (pushing Alekhine down into second). Alekhine stormed ostentatiously out of the hall.

When one member of the Cuban team, Francisco Planas, was crushed in just twenty moves with his king caught in the centre of the board, an annoyed Capablanca asked him: 'Why didn't you castle?' 'I couldn't, I didn't have time!' responded a flus-

Capablanca's tomb at Havana's Colón Cemetery is a very moving sight – it is in the form of a big white marble chess piece: a king of course.

tered Planas. 'What do you mean, you didn't have time? Show me the game.' As they went through the moves, Capa suddenly exclaimed: 'Stop right there. Right, *now* you can castle!' As the rest of the team looked at him in amazement, Capa added: 'Next time, you lose – but you castle!'

During the Olympiad there was a great deal of speculation over whether the rematch between Capablanca and Alekhine could somehow be arranged in Buenos Aires. There are two versions of what happened at this point. According to one, both men wrote to Arturo de Muro, president of the Argentinian Chess Federation, to suggest that they were willing, in principle, to meet each other again for the world title. The other version is very different: namely, that Carlos Querencio, who had been the arbiter in the original 1927 match in Buenos Aires, wrote to both Capa and Alekhine to propose the rematch. Capa replied positively, while Alekhine responded that he was unable to commit himself. This latter version seems to be the more accurate, since Querencio wrote an 'Open Letter to Alexander Alekhine,' published in the Buenos Aires newspaper, *Noticias Gráficas*, on September 19, 1939 – the day the Olympiad came to a close – accusing Alekhine of coming out with 'frequent excuses' every time Capablanca requested a rematch.

Querencio applauded Alekhine's patriotism but suggested that he play the match against Capa for the benefit of the French Red Cross. Alekhine never replied. Years later, Olga gave a very colourful account to Edward Winter, suggesting that Querencio went so far as to challenge Alekhine to a duel if he continued to deny Capa a rematch and that Alekhine fled into hiding in the bathroom.

There was reportedly one last chance. In October 1940, Alekhine was said to have sought permission to enter Cuba with the promise of playing the match with Capablanca. The Cuban authorities were said to have rejected the French-Russian's request.

On March 7, 1942, on a cold New York evening, Capablanca was cheerfully watching some friendly games taking place at the Manhattan Chess Club when he suddenly felt ill and asked for help in removing his coat. He collapsed shortly afterwards, from a cerebral haemorrhage, and although he was rushed to Mount Sinai Hospital, he died at six o'clock the following morning. The world was in shock. Mikhail Botvinnik declared that it was 'impossible to understand the world of chess without looking at it through the eyes of Capablanca.'

A frigate, the *José Marti*, was sent from Cuba to pick up Capa's body. Once back in Havana, it lay in state at the Capitolio Nacional in Havana. Guillermo Cabrera Infante was taken to view the body. He remembered later that his mother – who knew nothing about chess but all about Capablanca – said, as they stood looking over the coffin: 'He is one of Cuba's glories.' Not *was*, but *is*.

He received a burial with full honours at Havana's Colón Cemetery. His tomb is a very moving sight – it is in the form of a big white marble chess piece: a king, of course.

Capablanca was the last of the bohemian, playboy world chess champions. Olga always wanted to see a feature film based on her husband's life – and in a letter to Edward Winter in 1987 she said that the British actor Jeremy Brett would have been perfectly cast as Capa. In fact,

unbeknownst to Olga, there *was* a movie made about Capablanca just a year earlier: a Cuban film, called simply *Capablanca*, directed by Manuel Herrera and starring César Evora as Capa. Curiously, just like Pudovkin's silent comedy film, Herrera's movie is set in Moscow in 1925. Capablanca arrives to play chess – and finds love.

There are chess clubs named after Capablanca throughout Latin America but the famous Club Capablanca in Havana – in Calle Infanta number 54 – was restored and re-opened on the same spot as recently as April 2008. Visitors have included Anatoly Karpov. The museum contains a number of poignant reminders of a supreme chess career including the table and chairs used for Capa's match with Lasker in 1921. A perfume, called Capablanca, was even launched in 2008!

I will leave the last word to Capablanca's nemesis. Alexander Alekhine, who survived him by only four years, declared: 'There never was, and there never will be, a genius to touch him.' ■

ADAM FEINSTEIN is currently working on a book about cultural policy in Cuba since the Revolution. His biography, Pablo Neruda: A Passion for Life, *was published by Bloomsbury in the UK and the USA in 2004. His latest book,* A History of Autism: Conversations with the Pioneers, *was published by Wiley-Blackwell in the UK and the USA in 2010.*

Food for thought from Plovdiv

In the past years Plovdiv has established itself as a leading chess destination. Many European top events have taken place in Bulgaria's second largest city, including the European Team Championship in 2003 and the European Club Cup in 2010. The most prestigious event, the European Individual Championship, was held in Plovdiv in 2008, and this year a jaw-dropping field that included 180 GMs arrived for the 13th edition. Russia's Dmitry Jakovenko claimed the title with an impressive hat-trick in the final three rounds. Dejan Bojkov reports from Plovdiv, where the zero-tolerance rule and a new anti-draw measure caused a lot of commotion and frustration.

T

Tradition is Plovdiv's main weapon when it comes to chess. It is not only the city in Bulgaria that has produced the most GMs, it also owns a famous chess school and various strong clubs. There is also a lot of experience in organizing big events. The spacious halls in the Novotel Hotel provided good playing facilities, and above all quick access, especially for those players that stayed in the hotel. For those who didn't, there were plenty of hotels and apartments for rent within walking distance from the venue. The city is easily accessible, has an airport and is situated less than 150 kilometres away from the capital Sofia.

A positive sign before the start of the event was the co-operation of the

ELENA KLIMETS

Eltaj Safarli and Tal Baron cannot believe that their game has ended in 0-0. Neither can Shakhriyar Mamedyarov (second from left).

ACP, the Association of Chess Players, with the organizers. ACP-members received special conditions: a 50 per cent discount on the organization fee and an additional 5 per cent off the room rates at the official championship hotel, the already mentioned Novotel. Reigning European Champion Vladimir Potkin from Russia received a special invitation to defend his title, with all expenses paid by the organizers. An excellent idea, showing respect for the champion!

On a negative note, the prize-fund was decreased (this time € 100,000 in total) compared to the previous two years. Besides the money prizes, the participants competed for twenty-three tickets to the next World Cup.

A seed for future problems was planted with two rules in the tour-nament regulations. To begin with: 'Communication between players (the offer of a draw) is forbidden until the 40th move has been played.' And furthermore: 'The zero-tolerance rule will be applied for each round.'

While the latter has been applied at various mass events, the former had not been tested yet. The relative obscurity of the rule and especially its incompatibility with the FIDE rules of the threefold repetition would cause the biggest controversies of the event.

Another novelty was the introduction of a dress code. To cut a long story short, I will limit myself by mentioning what is inappropriate to wear during the games: beach-wear, slippers, hats or caps (except for religious purposes) and anything that might be ugly or disrespectful to the audience or one's opponent. Additionally, according to the regulations, the winners were kindly invited to wear suits at the closing ceremony. The arbiters had their own dress code.

The tournament attracted 180 GMs from 39 countries and a total of 293 participants. Fifteen of them were rated above 2700. At 2767, Fabiano Caruana from Italy was the rating favourite.

The first rounds showed that the days of easy wins for the highest-rated players are irretrievably behind us. Some of the favourites were facing GMs as early as Round 1 and many of them lost points at the start. Still, many of the top guns had a lot to show:

Sutovsky-Grigoriants
position after 31...♕d5

Former European champion and ACP President Emil Sutovsky was close to winning the title in Plovdiv four years ago. This year he did not do that well, but still managed to produce some beautiful chess. Have a look at the following combination:

32.♖e8+! ♔h7 Of course 32...♖xe8 fails to 33.♖xe8+ ♖xe8 34.♕xd5. **33.♖1e5!!** Interference. The queen will now lack access to the h5 square. **33...♘xe5** As 33...♕xf3 runs into 34.♖h5 mate. **34.♘f6+** And Black resigned in view of 34...gxf6 35.♕h5+ ♔g7 36.♕h8 mate.

Chess remains the only sport that allows a player to compete even if he is injured. Bulgarian grandmaster Kiril Georgiev broke his hand one day before the start of the championship, but nevertheless played, scoring plus four and almost qualifying for the World Cup.

While some of the rating favourites were recovering from a poor start, the Englishman Gawain Jones took the lead with four straight wins.

Round 6 saw the first tension caused by the new rules. Here is the reason:

SL 11.16 – D10
Sergey Volkov
Alexey Dreev
Plovdiv 2012 (6)

1.d4 d5 2.c4 c6 3.♘c3 ♘f6 4. cxd5 cxd5 5.♗f4 ♘c6 6.e3 a6 7.♗d3 ♗g4 8.♘ge2 e6 9.♕b3 ♘a5 10.♕a4+ ♘c6 11.♕b3 ♘a5 12.♕a4+ ♘c6 13.♕b3
Draw.

A draw on move 13. Despite the prohibition of the draw offer Volkov and Dreev simply repeated the position three times, and without communicating with each other signed the score sheets. In the previous rounds, some players forgot about the new draw offer rules and offered draws at an early stage. However, after being reminded about the regulations they continued to play until move 40. This game showed a flaw in the regulations and raised a tough question: was the prohibition of offering a draw before move 40 of a higher order than the FIDE rules?!

Anyway, this was minor news compared to the forfeit of six Georgian players and one Greek girl (of Georgian origin) that same day. They fell victim to the beginning of the daylight-saving time the night before. The clocks were moved one hour forward, and despite repeated warning by the arbiters in six different languages, the Georgians failed to appear in time for the round. The meagre excuse they had was that Georgia does not have daylight-saving time. Their two top players – Baadur Jobava and Levan Pantsulaia – did arrive in time, however. Perhaps an explanation for their ignorance can be found in language barriers.

After the free day Round 7 saw the emergence of a new leader. The Belorussian grandmaster Sergey Azarov defeated German grandmaster Arkadij Naiditsch to take the sole lead. However, the top spot seemed too hot to stay on for more than one game, as in the coming rounds the leaders changed constantly.

The seventh round was also the round in which second seed Shakhriyar Mamedyarov finally achieved a whole point after six consecutive draws. However, Round 8 had barely started when the Azeri grandmaster saw his hopes of fighting back vanish in thin air when he appeared late for the game and lost due to the zero tolerance rule. As a curious detail we can mention that his opponent, Shota Azaladze, was one of the forfeited Georgian players in Round 6. Mamedyarov complained on Twitter that he had arrived 10 seconds late. The arbiters claimed it was more than a minute.

All of this does not matter as long as there is a rule. I spoke with my colleagues about their views on this rule and almost all of them are against it. They are less reluctant if the rule is applied in a tournament that can host all the players in the same hotel or at top tournaments with a small number of participants. But in a mass event some tolerance is needed. Fifteen minutes for example. Instead of a direct forfeit many participants suggested a penalty system similar to the one that is applied at the Russian team championships. You are five minutes late, or 10, or, say, a maximum of 15 minutes? No problem, pay your penalty and keep on playing. You do not want to pay your penalty? Then you deserve to be forfeited. Thus both the organizers and the participants will be happy.

In the meantime, Vladimir Malakhov won a fine positional game against Azarov and replaced him in the lead. He was joined at the top of the table by Vladimir Akopian and the pleasant surprise of the event Maxim Matlakov from Russia, who edged out Victor Bologan.

Round 9 was a sad day for the players. It was on this day that a new result was introduced in tournament practice: 0-0. Not referring to castling kingside, but describing an actual result. Maybe an inspired attempt to fight rating inflation? This is what happened in the game Baron-Safarli:

> 'Despite repeated warning in six languages, the Georgians failed to appear in time.'

CA 5.6 – E06
Tal Baron
Eltaj Safarli
Plovdiv 2012 (9)

1.d4 ♘f6 2.c4 e6 3.g3 d5 4.♘f3 ♗e7 5.♗g2 0-0 6.0-0 dxc4 7.♕c2 a6 8.♕xc4 b5 9.♕c2 ♗b7 10. ♗d2 ♗e4 11.♕c1 ♗b7 12.♕c2 ♗e4 13.♕c1 ♗b7 14.♕c2 0-0.

Formally, the players' sin was that they did not claim the draw in accordance with the rules. They just signed the score sheet after the repetition without asking the arbiter and left the score sheets on the board. While the shocked players were protesting against the result of their game to the Executive Director of the ECU, Vladimir Sakotic, in the foyer, the players on Board 1, Akopian and Malakhov, left the venue in a good mood. Their game lasted 16 moves, but the draw was made in accordance with the rules.

Baron and Safarli wrote a protest which was dismissed: 'The appellants did not follow article 9.2 saying that the player (Baron in this case) should first write his move on his score sheet (which he did) and declare to the arbiter his intention to make this move (which he also did, but only after both players had written down a draw as the game's result, signed the score sheets and even arranged the pieces back to their initial positions). By doing this the players decided in fact deliberately to finish the game before the 40th move without the approval of the arbiters.'

The bitterness of the atmosphere was highlighted by Mamedyarov's decision in this round to offer a draw to his opponent on move nineteen, without even repeating the moves:

KI 20.2 – E90
Alvar Alonso Rosell
Shakhriyar Mamedyarov
Plovdiv 2012 (9)

1.d4 g6 2.c4 ♗g7 3.e4 d6 4.♘c3 ♘f6 5.♘f3 0-0 6.h3 c5 7.d5 b5 8. cxb5 a6 9.a4 ♘bd7 10.♖b1 axb5 11.axb5 ♘b6 12.♗e2 e6 13.dxe6 ♗xe6 14.0-0 d5 15.exd5 ♘bxd5 16.♘xd5 ♘xd5 17.♗g5 ♕b6 18.♕d2 ♘c7 19.♗h6 ♘xb5 0-0.

The draw offer was accepted by his opponent and both players received a zero. Afterwards there was speculation that the Azeri GM had made a protest this way to support his compatriot Safarli. Closer to the truth was that Mamedyarov had enough of the tournament, and did not want to lose more rating points. For some reason he thought that the 0-0 result would not be calculated for his rating. Wrong! It will be and both players will lose rating points. As for his opponent, he simply did not know that the additional rules did not allow him to make a draw.

Mamedyarov withdrew from the tournament, but stated that he had no bad feelings towards the organiz-

ers and the arbiters. Safarli followed his example, but felt robbed: 'It does not make sense. One day they say one thing, the next day another. Why can't I make a draw when there is a three-fold repetition? Why do I need to ask the arbiter for permission?'

As the tournament progressed, the players became cleverer in (dis)obeying the new rules. The game Jankovic-Lysyj saw a seven-minute draw of 41 moves, while in the game Maze-Smirin the players started to repeat moves on move 16. Reluctant to ask the arbiter for permission to draw they instead decided to repeat the position until move forty (24 times...). Things like that...

Against the dark background of these incidents many people missed the appearance of a new bright talent. Fifteen-year-old Kiril Alekseenko of Russia achieved a GM norm and won the first special prize for performance. There was something symbolic in

the fact that he made the norm in his game against his compatriot and now former European champion Vladimir Potkin.

Here is a fragment of Alekseenko's play:

Volkov-Alekseenko
position after 27.♘f4

27...♗b4! A nice shot. The threat of ...♕h7 leaves White no time to react. **28.♘xc7** White is getting mated after 28.axb4 ♕h7 29.♔f1 ♘xe3+ 30. fxe3 ♕xc2. **28...♗xa5 29.♘xa6+** ♔a8 White resigned.

While some players were punished for making short draws, two Turkish players created an absolute record in EICC history. The game Vahap Sanal-Emre Can lasted 228 moves and a little less than eight hours! I immediately thought that this would be a good tie-break criterion in a tournament stimulating fighting chess. However, my colleagues quickly defused my ingenuity. Indeed, can one blame a player if he is a sharp tactician and mates his opponents quickly, or if he manages to create an early perpetual when he is low on material? Nah, it does not work. But I still love the idea to stimulate, rather than to punish. I liked what I saw in Australia, the so-called fighting fund. It is a bit complicated, but the essence is that the organizers offer additional prizes for the top players who do not make short draws until move 30 throughout the whole event and win their final games.

On that same fateful day the games on the top three boards ended peace-

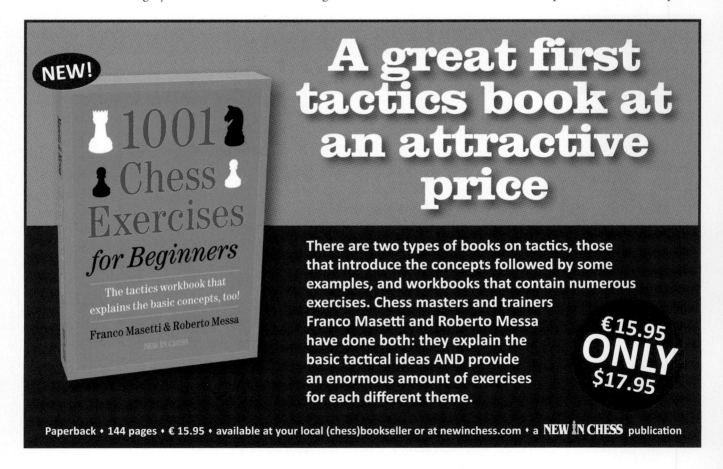

fully, thus allowing four more players to join the leaders. The situation was heating up and required nerves of steel from the medal contenders. In Round 10 only one of them managed to strike.

NI 12.9 – E14
Laurent Fressinet
Vladimir Akopian
Plovdiv 2012 (10)

1.d4 ♘f6 2.♘f3 e6 3.c4 b6 4.e3 ♗b7 5.♘c3 ♗b4 6.♗d3 0-0 7.0-0 ♗xc3

In this position 7...d5 and 7...c5 are more common continuations.

8.bxc3 d6

8...♗e4 was tried by Hikaru Nakamura. Fressinet opined that Black should go 8...♘e4, for example: 9.♘e1 f5 10.f3 ♘g5 11.♕e2 ♕f6 12.♘c2 d6 13.a4 ♘c6 14.♗a3 ♕g6, with unclear play as in Gelfand-Vallejo, Leon 2010. **9. ♘d2 ♘bd7 10.e4 e5 11.f3 ♖e8 12.♖f2** White frees the f1 square for the knight.

12...c6?!

Fressinet considered himself lucky when Akopian chose this dubious plan. Technically speaking, this move is a novelty. Here Black has tried 12...♘f8 13.♘f1 ♘e6 (or 13...♘g6) 14.♗c2 c5, hoping to fix the centre. However, after 15.♗a4 ♖f8 16.dxe5! dxe5 17.♖d2 ♕c7 18.♘e3 White establishes his knight on d5, as Botvinnik loved to do in this pawn structure, and enjoys an edge, as in Aloma-Mascaro, Son Servera 2004. **13.♘f1 d5** The problem with this plan is that the game is opened for the white bishop's pleasure. **14.♘g3 ♕c7** White is also

clearly better after 14...exd4 15.cxd4 dxc4 16.♗xc4. **15.♗g5!** Enticing the black h-pawn to a vulnerable square. **15...h6 16.♗e3 ♖ad8 17.♘f5**

The sacrifice on h6 is already in the air. White only needs to bring the queen to d2.

17...dxc4?! Setting free the bishop. Also bad was 17...♗c8 18.♕d2 dxe4 19.♗xh6 exd3 (on 19...g6, 20.fxe4 is crushing) 20.♗xg7 ♘h7 21.♕h6, winning.
However, 17...♘f8 was to be preferred. **18.♗xc4 b5 19.♗b3 ♘c5 20. ♖d2 ♘xb3** This loses practically by force. **21.axb3 a6 22.dxe5! ♖xd2 23.♕xd2 ♕xe5**
Or 23...♖xe5 24.♖d1 ♔h7 (if 24...♖e8 25.♘xg7! ♔xg7 26.♗xh6+ ♔h7 27.♕g5 ♖g8 28.♕h4, winning) 25.♗f4 ♕b6+ 26.♔h1 ♖e8 27.♗xh6, and White wins.
24.♗d4 ♕e6

25.♘xh6+! ♔h7 After 25...gxh6 26.♕xh6 Black has to give his queen to avoid direct mate. **26.♘f5** Black resigned.

After a lucky win in the previous round, when Timofeev blundered an

exchange in an approximately equal position, Dmitry Jakovenko knocked his compatriot Mikhail Kobalia out of the fight for the medals. Jakovenko sacrificed a piece for two pawns and created a nice pawn mass on the queen's flank.

Let us not forget that the championship also included a battle for 23 qualifying spots for the World Cup. In some of the key games, nerves were the decisive factor. Sometimes the need to play for a win inspired the players to go for extreme measures.

NI 22.11 – E38
Momchil Nikolov
Ivan Ivanisevic
Plovdiv 2012 (10)

1.d4 ♘f6 2.c4 e6 3.♘c3 ♗b4 4.♕c2 c5 5.dxc5 ♘a6 6.a3 ♗xc3+ 7.♕xc3 ♘xc5 8.f3 d5 9. cxd5 b6 10.b4 ♘a4 11.♕c2 b5 12.e4 a6

13.dxe6
A novelty.
13...♗xe6 14.♕c6+ ♘d7 15.♗g5

15...♕xg5!!
It is not every day that you see a double-rook sacrifice in modern chess.

However, this line had been examined by the Serbian GM some time ago.

16.♕xa8+ ♚e7 17.♕xh8

Ivanisevic said he seemed to remember that 17.♕a7 is the best move and that it should lead to a forced draw.

17...♕e3+

18.♗e2

It looks as if White loses after 18.♗e2 ♘b2 19.♖d1 ♘xd1 20.♚xd1 ♗b3+ 21.♚e1 ♘e5, with mate to follow. But instead of 20.♚xd1 he has the resource 20.♕xg7! ♘f2 21.♕c3 ♘d3+ 22.♚d1 ♘f2+ 23.♚e1, and Black

cannot play for a win, as in the line 23...♕xc3+ 24.♘xc3 ♘xh1 25.♗e2 the black knight is trapped.

18...♕c3+ 19.♚f2 ♕d4+! 20.♚f1!

Or otherwise it is mate after 20.♚g3 ♘f6 21.♖d1 ♘h5+ 22.♚h4 ♕f6+ 23.♚xh5 ♕h6 mate.

20...♕xa1+ 21.♚f2

21...♕d4+

Had Ivanisevic checked his analyses before the game, he would probably have played the nice 21...♘c3! 22.♕a8 (22.♕xg7 ♘xe4+) 22...♘xe2 23.♘xe2

(23.♚xe2 ♗c4+ – 23...♕b2+!?, followed by ...♕xg2, is not bad either – 24.♚f2 ♕f1+ 25.♚g3 ♕e1+ 26.♚f4 h6! wins for Black) 23...♕xh1, and Black is clearly on top.

22.♚f1 h6 23.g4 ♘c3

Black's attack is more than dangerous and after a lot of action and drama he managed to convert the advantage.

Going into the last round, Laurent Fressinet was the sole leader, half a point ahead of a chasing pack of nine players. In his final game, the Frenchman had to face the highest-rated of those nine, Dmitry Jakovenko. Fortune was leading the Russian GM to the title. As in the penultimate round, he was once again lifted to play against a direct rival who had more points than him. And again he was playing with the white pieces. Jakovenko knew that a draw would be good enough for a medal, but naturally he wanted to win one of a more precious metal.

NOTES BY
Dmitry Jakovenko

NI 27.9 – D38
Dmitry Jakovenko
Laurent Fressinet
Plovdiv 2012 (11)

Before the game Fressinet and I had the best tie-breaks in the tournament, so that a win would guarantee me first place, and a draw would give it to my opponent. Moreover, a draw would probably give me the silver or bronze medal – it was unlikely that there would be two decisive games in my points group. Therefore I was quite unable to determine for myself the degree of permissible risk, especially since the prohibition on draw offers before the 40th move did not allow me to resort to this saving measure in the event of danger.

1.d4
For a start I place a pawn on a defended square.
1...d5 2.c4 e6 3.♘c3 ♗b4 4.♘f3 ♘f6
What is meant by luck in chess? For example, it is when in a decisive game your opponent 'guesses' precisely that opening which you analysed immediately before the tournament.
5.cxd5 exd5 6.♗g5 ♘bd7 7.e3 c5 8.dxc5 ♕a5 9.♖c1

When in 2009 Kramnik won with this variation against Ponomariov, it looked like an idea for one game. It is sufficient to say that the next time this position occurred was six months later, and again in a Kramnik game.

On this occasion the victim was Mamedyarov, who obviously did not expect a repetition. After this everyone began playing it, and now it is virtually the most topical line of the Ragozin Defence.
9...♗xc3+
Both of Kramnik's white games went 9...♘e4 10.♕xd5 ♘xc3 11.bxc3 ♗xc3+ 12.♔d1. But with black against Anish Giri (Amber 2011) it was 9...♗xc3+ that Vladimir preferred.
10.bxc3 0-0 11.♘d4 ♕xc5 12.♗d3
In my preparations I was more expecting a Queen's Gambit or Slav Defence, and therefore at this point I could no longer remember my notes and I began playing spontaneously. The first question is – where to place the bishop? At d3 it may be attacked by the knight from e5 or c5, but at e2 it is more passively placed, and in addition, after 12.♗e2 White cannot castle on his next move on account of ...♘e4, ...♘xc3 and ...♘xe2. It was this last consideration that determined my choice – and it turned out that no one has played any differently here.

12...♖e8
In Wijk aan Zee 2011, the interesting game Nakamura-Grischuk was played: 12...♘e4 13.♗f4 ♘b6 14.♕c2 h6 15.f3 ♘f6 16.g4!? ♖e8 17.♔f2!? ♘c4 18.h4!?. Unexpectedly finding himself under the threat of a direct attack on his king, Alexander decided on the sacrifice 18...♗xg4, but his initiative proved insufficient for equality – Hikaru won.
13.0-0 ♘e4 14.♗f4

14...♘e5?!
It is with this that Black's problems in the game begin. The c3-c4 break should have been prevented. Since after the natural 14...♘b6 there is the unpleasant 15.♘b5 ♗e7 16.c4!, he should have preferred 14...♘d6.
15.♗xe5 ♖xe5 16.c4

It is quite possible that Laurent underestimated the danger of this position. It appears that in the absence of any weaknesses Black should be able to gradually defend. But it transpires that the need to spend tempi on the retreat of his hanging pieces and problems in finding good squares for the c8-bishop make the defence very unpleasant.

But for me, beginning from this moment, a new psychological problem arose: after obtaining a position without any risk of losing, from an over-nervous state I passed into an over-quiet one and I was constantly forced to remind myself that I needed a win, and not simply a comfortable advantage.
16...♘f6
The knight would have been better placed on c5, or at least on d6. But

continued on page 36

Dmitry Jakovenko: 'I want to get back on the team!'

Vladimir Barsky

The chess world loves myths. It spawns them itself, then cultivates them until they become 'well-known facts' – and it's extremely difficult to part with them. One of them is that Alexander Nikitin had been preparing a 'second Kasparov' for a long time, who would surpass the first one (with whom the coach had fallen out at that point), and then suddenly he went and talked him out of chess as a profession!

For a decade and a half, from the late '70s until 1992, Alexander Sergeevich Nikitin headed the Tigran Petrosian School (after the ninth World Champion's untimely death – the Petrosian Memorial School). In its last years its sessions attracted a real cast of stars: Sasha Grischuk, Volodya Malakhov, Levon Aronian, Baadur Jobava, Maxim Turov... Meanwhile, the experienced coach particularly singled out Mitya Jakovenko, claiming that he was surpassing Kasparov's improvement rate and travelling to Siberia to work with him. But when the young man finished school, Nikitin supposedly talked his pupil out of playing chess professionally. Instead of that he advised him that it would be better to get a good education and do something else with his life. Why, since his pupil's results were unswervingly heading upwards? Either the coach was fed up with chess, which had entered the era of knockout championships, or he'd made peace with Kasparov...

This mystery wasn't difficult to solve, just by asking Nikitin or Jakovenko about it, as there were ample opportunities. But... I heard this story from different people so often (with slight variations) that I completely believed its authenticity!

Dmitry Jakovenko was born on June 28, 1983 in Omsk – a fairly large city in Western Siberia, where, for example, Vitaly Tseshkovsky and Konstantin Landa are from. Soon afterwards the Jakovenko family moved to Nizhnevartovsk – a big oil-producing centre in the Khanty-Mansiysk region. His father was a construction engineer and his mother was a doctor. Mitya's dad, a strong amateur, taught him chess: he enjoyed correspondence chess and taught his young son as well. At the age of seven Mitya became a first category player, and at 14 an international master. He graduated from school with a gold medal and was keen on the exact sciences, maths and physics; he was the winner of the Siberian mathematical Olympiad. He easily got into a prestigious Moscow university, the department of pure maths and cybernetics.

Dmitry has always given the impression that he's a very easy-going, sociable, cheerful person who isn't self-absorbed. I remember how during the Super Final of the 2004 Russian Championship (where he wasn't playing) he constantly came into the press centre, enthusiastically analysed with journalists, and once even took the role of demonstrator – he helped Garry Kasparov demonstrate a game he'd just played. He learnt from others and didn't have any issues about that! And within two years he himself was sharing first place in the championship of the country, although he lost the additional match to Alekseev. It was around the same time that Jakovenko got onto the Russian team and solidly secured himself at its 'base'. A player of the classical positional style, as a rule he performs very successfully in team tournaments. He loses very rarely, and he can beat anyone.

In 2007 Jakovenko helped his friend Alexander Grischuk in the Candidates' matches in Elista. Alexander returned from the Kalmyk capital with a ticket to the World Championship in Mexico, and Dmitry with a young bride! True, after getting married Jakovenko had a slight decline in his sporting results, but he himself isn't keen to establish a causal link between these two events – he self-critically says that his rating at the time of 2760 (5th place in the world, by the way!) didn't completely objectively reflect his real playing strength, so a certain decline was inevitable.

I've known Jakovenko for a very long time, since he used to stop by the offices of '64' as a teenager. A photograph

ELENA KLIMETS

A photo from the 64 archives. Alexander Nikitin and Dmitry Jakovenko are studying a position in the office of the late Alexander Roshal.

VLADIMIR BARSKY

that I took is stored in the archives, in which he and Nikitin are examining some game or other in Roshal's office. But I never got around to interviewing Dmitry before. Now there was an excellent reason to do so: Jakovenko had won the European Championship in Plovdiv outright. The first question, naturally, was about how the battle went.

'As in all Swisses, nothing in particular happened right up until the last rounds, when the battle for the highest places began. For me the tournament turned out to be a little challenging: I almost lost in the third round and just about won in the sixth, but after getting through very bad time-trouble – I had about five minutes left for 15 moves. In the seventh round I had to find precise moves for a long time in order to extinguish Cheparinov's initiative. Then I won a pawn, but blundered it back in time-trouble, and it ended up as a draw.

'The last game, with Fressinet, also turned out to be tough, of course. I got an advantage fairly quickly, and without any risk of losing. A draw would almost certainly have given me second or third place. But I was trying to "get myself going", thinking, in a position like this I shouldn't be satisfied with a draw, I have to look for a win! In the endgame Fressinet missed a small tactic and was left a pawn down, after which it wasn't too difficult to make the best of my advantage.'

The conditions at the championship were more stressful than usual? From the zero tolerance for being late, to the draws before 40 moves?

'I didn't notice any of that. Yes, there was lateness, associated with the clocks going forward for spring. It's a mystery to me why they don't have a rest day on that Sunday. This is the second time that the clocks have gone forward at the European Championship on a playing day. It's strange!

'As for the ban on draws, I don't see any problems there. You can't agree a draw before the 40th move, but no one is stopping you from repeating the position three times. But some people signed their score-sheets without even establishing a threefold repetition. I think that they themselves were heading for a "0-0".'

You started playing when you could be up to 59 minutes late and it was possible to agree a draw even on the first move. Doesn't the current trend bother you?

'I don't like the situation with the ban on being late, of course. I don't see the point of it. You could understand it if we were talking about a round-robin tournament. But why introduce it as a compulsory rule everywhere?

'As for the ban on draws, although I like agreeing a draw, I support the innovation, because there really is an artificial point here where you can agree a draw in a difficult position. People tell me very often: but if the position is absolutely drawn, then why keep playing it until the 40th move? I reply: then you can go ♔g1-h1-g1 and let your opponent know that you want to make a draw. And if you can't allow yourself to stay still, it means the position isn't that drawn yet and you have

to keep playing. I don't see any problems here.

'The fact that it increases the burden on players is another matter. Perhaps in these conditions you need two rest days instead of one for 11 rounds.'

The burden increases, yes, but the prize fund decreases. By comparison with what it was five or six years ago.

'I think that the decrease in the prize fund actually took place this year. In Dresden and Aix-les-Bains first prize was 20,000 euros last year. I just don't know how quickly the prizes went down after that. This year, certainly, the prize fund has been reduced significantly.'

Do you see Nikitin at the moment?

'A day after I got back from Plovdiv, Alexander Sergeevich was already visiting me, congratulating me on my victory. We live close to each other now, a 10-minute car journey away, so no problems with seeing each other arise.'

Does your first coach have a strong influence on you?

'In principle, yes. But I have to say that my first coach was my dad – until I was 10 or 11, and he also had quite a large influence on me. Alexander Sergeevich helped me in the next stage. A youth coach, you could say. But his influence was also great, of course.'

Is it true that Nikitin talked you out of playing chess professionally?

'No, that didn't happen. He talked me out of giving up my studies in favour of chess, he argued that I should get a good education.'

Was he right?

'I think, in my case, yes. I won't speak for other players, as each one has their own situation.'

Studying at university didn't interfere with your chess development?

'In my case it didn't interfere because in any case I didn't work on my chess eight hours a day. So I had enough time to study at university too, and I can't say that my studies were all that difficult or took away a great deal of my time. I also travelled to events easily, there were no big problems with that. But I repeat: everyone has their own situation, there's no way I'd want to say that it would be the same for everyone, or that everyone should absolutely have to go to university.'

Is maths closely connected to chess? Many people think that they're completely different things.

'Perhaps maths is closer to the final stage of a chess game, when you sometimes have to calculate either a mating combination or a win in the endgame or an accurate draw. This is somewhat similar to solving a mathematical problem, where you also have to strictly prove some kind of hypothesis without missing the slightest detail. It's the same in chess: finding the strict solution to a position without missing anything. I'm considered quite good at playing specifically the last part of the game. Perhaps my mathematical bent helps me with that. Certainly, in positions that are amenable to precise calculation I make mistakes rather infrequently – if I have time to think, of course. I sit down, immerse myself in the position and calculate it to the end.

'At the same time, in the opening and the transition to the middlegame the positions are too complicated to be calculated, and here there's probably little in common with maths.'

It seemed that in the past few years you had something of a decline – after a sharp ascent. What was that due to?

'I don't completely understand which years you're talking about. My rating peak was in 2009, and to talk bluntly about a decline, when I quite confidently held my rating in the vicinity of 2720-2730... For me it's a mystery why everyone thinks that I've been in a crisis for the past two years. If it's not a crisis, then what – I should fight for the championship title?

'The law of dialectics says that development takes place in leaps: accumulation is a leap. I was in the accumulation stage. Perhaps I'm still in it now. I think I'm playing now at approximately the same strength that I was playing at three years ago. And the fact that I got up to 2760 back then was to some extent conditioned by the course of events, good endings to games. Especially as in chess two half-points saved are equivalent to 10 rating points. This all took place quite quickly, especially as I was playing in rather a lot of tournaments at the time. A leap up or down can take place easily, and very many people have these leaps.'

You don't feel there's a shortage of tournaments?

'Last year I played 80 games – which means there's no such shortage. It was another matter three years ago, when I had invitations to super-tournaments, to the European Championship, and I might not have gone. But now I have to! Although I don't have big problems with that.'

Did the fact that you stopped being invited to play on the team become an additional nuisance?

'There was a possibility of leaving me off the team. I wasn't 100-percent certain to be on the team on the basis of objective indices. I think I missed playing for the team twice – at the last World Team Championship and the European. Certainly, if I was going to be picked then it would have been for fourth board or as a reserve, and there were several candidates with roughly equal claims. I can't say that I was offended because they didn't pick me – that was the coach's right. But, of course, I didn't like it. Naturally I want to play for the team, and I've always wanted to, I've never refused. Of course I want to get back on the team! ∎

continued from page 31

Black has no choice. If 16...♕e7, in order to free the c5-square for the knight, 17.f4! wins immediately, while in reply to 16...♘d6 there follows 17. ♘b3, and 17...♘c6 18.cxd5 ♕xd5 is impossible, again because of 19.f4!. Black is forced to play 17...♕a3 18. cxd5 ♕xa2, but here White's passed pawns are obviously more dangerous than Black's.

Finally, it is also not possible simply to develop the bishop: after 16...♗d7 17.♘b3 ♕e7 18.f4! ♖f5 19.♘d4 dxc4 20.♘xf5 ♗xf5 21.♗xc4 ♖d8 22.♕a4 Black loses the exchange without sufficient compensation.

17.♕b3

17.cxd5 ♕xd5 18.♗c4 looks tempting, but the accurate 18...♕d7! (bad is 18...♕d8 19.♘f3 ♖e8 20.♕xd8 ♖xd8 21.♘g5) 19.♕b3 ♕e7 enables Black to consolidate.

17...♖e7

During the game it was difficult to play 17...♕b6 and agree to a cheerless endgame after 18.c5 ♕xb3 19.axb3. But now, knowing the result of the game, it seems to me that here White has that 'comfortable advantage' which may prove insufficient for a win.

18.♖fd1

18...♗g4?

There would appear to be no concrete threats, but on every move Black has to beware of losing by force – and this is very tiring. Laurent attempts to change the pattern of the play, but objectively his idea is bad. However, I wouldn't presume to suggest something instead. During the game 18...

dxc4 19.♗xc4 ♕h5 seemed the most natural to me, and I was intending to reply 20.f3 followed by e3-e4, retaining strong pressure.

19.f3 ♗e6 20.cxd5 ♕xd5 21.♗c4 ♕e5

22.f4?

Although the real mistake came later, it is this move that deserves a question mark, signifying that White failed to see a winning continuation.

Correct was 22.♘xe6 fxe6 23.f4 ♕f5 24.♖d6 ♖ae8 25.♗b5! ♘e4 (if the rook moves there follows 26.♗d3,

Dmitry Jakovenko: 'I am afraid that, apart from the banal "I was very glad" (very happy would be an exaggeration), I have nothing to say.'

winning the e6-pawn – I didn't see this pendulum manoeuvre) 26.♖d4 ♘c5 27.♕a3 ♖c8 28.♕xa7, winning a pawn with an overwhelming position. The variation is not so complicated, and this was a very annoying flaw in an otherwise good game.

22...♕e4

I was in no great doubt that the endgame after 22...♗xc4 23.fxe5 ♗xb3 24.exf6 ♗xd1 25.fxe7 ♗a4 would seem too dangerous to my opponent, but everything is not so simple, and in this case I would have had to find 26.♖c7 b6 27.♔f2! g6 28.♔f3 ♔g7 29.♔e4 ♔f6 30.♔d5, which should win.

23.♘xe6 fxe6

It was not yet too late to revert to the winning variation by 24.♖d4 ♕f5 25.♖d6, but the move 22.f4 was made with a different idea.

24.♗e2

I thought that the threat to the b7-pawn would force Black to play 24...♕g6 (heading for f7), after which 25.♖c5 gives an enormous advantage. But there followed...

24...♘d5 25.♔f2 ♕b4

It was this move that I had missed. Very fortunately for me, the exchange of queens still does not solve all Black's problems.

26.♗c4 ♕xb3 27.♗xb3 ♘c7 28. ♖c5

White's immediate threats have been parried, but the defence remains difficult. The advance of the queenside pawns will merely lead to their loss, due to the weakness of the e6-pawn Black cannot hope to activate his knight, and meanwhile White is planning an offensive with his h- and g-pawns.

28...♔f8

It is obvious that at this moment Black

had not yet decided whether to place his pawn on g6, as otherwise he would have done this without losing time.

29.♖e5 g6

The constant threat of f4-f5 was highly unpleasant, but now White acquires a new target to attack.

30.h4 ♔g7 31.h5 ♖f8 32.g4

32...♖ff7

In reply to 32...gxh5 33.♖xh5 e5 there would have followed 34.♖dh1 ♔h8 35.♗c2 (here too the computer makes a correction: 35.g5! exf4 36.g6 wins immediately) 35...♖ff7 36.f5, with an overwhelming advantage.

With the move in the game Black has created the threat of ...♖d7 – the exchange of a pair of rooks would greatly ease his task. The endgame after 33.♔f3 ♖d7 34.♖xd7 ♖xd7 35. ♗xe6 ♖e7 36.♗b3 ♖xe5 37.fxe5 may turn out not to be won. And again luck was on my side – during 3-4 minutes of my remaining ten I managed to find a way of forestalling the opponent's idea.

33.♖g5! ♖d7?

Laurent does not see my idea. He should have continued defending passively. However, it is possible that objectively the position is already indefensible.

34.hxg6 hxg6

35.♗c2! Winning the g6-pawn and with it the game.

35...♔f8

If 35...♖xd1 White wins by 36. ♖xg6+ ♔h7 37.♖xe6+ ♔h8 38.♖h6+ ♔g7 39.♖g6+ ♔h8 40.♗xd1.

36.♖xg6 ♖xd1 37.♗xd1 ♖h7

By beginning an advance of his passed pawns – 37... b5 – Black could still have maintained the intrigue, but I should like to think that I would have coped with my excitement and converted the game to a win.

38.♗b3 ♔e7 39.f5

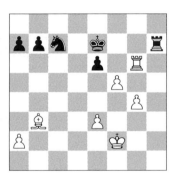

Now it is all very simple.

39...exf5 40.gxf5 ♘e8 41.e4 ♘d6 42.f6+ Black resigned.

A natural conclusion to the commentary would be a description of my feelings after the game. I am afraid that, apart from the banal 'I was very glad' (very happy would be an exaggeration), I have nothing to say.

Within a few weeks there will be a new tournament (the Russian club championship), and at the board the title of European champion will not be of any use to me ☺.

■ ■ ■

In the last round, Boards 2, 4 and 5 ended in relatively eventless draws. The last pair that kept on fighting was Inarkiev and Vallejo. 'I blundered badly in the opening', said Vallejo after the game. 'My preparation was a little bit of this and a little bit of that and I did not decide what to play until I sat over the board. I was lucky to save the game.' Less lucky was his opponent, who shared second place but remained three performance points behind the bronze medallist. Even less lucky was Dmitry Andreikin, whose performance was a mere point less than the winner of the bronze medal.

It was Vladimir Malakhov who grabbed bronze, his third medal after the two silvers from Budva and Istanbul. Humble and extremely strong, the Russian GM probably lacks the necessary aggression for the title. One cannot help but remember the famous case in Istanbul, when he allowed Zurab Azmaiparashvili to take back a losing move, a generous gesture that cost Malakhov the title.

The silver medal was for Laurent Fressinet. Except for the last game, he played an excellent tournament and this was his major success at a European championships so far.

And so the title went to Russia. Dmitry Jakovenko had some lesser results for a while and it is good to see him back in top form.

An amusing tradition at the EICC was kept alive. For the 13th year in a row, none of the previous winners managed to win the title for a second time.

'At the board the title of European champion will not be of any use to me ☺'

NOTES BY
Laurent Fressinet

GI 2.3 – D73
Laurent Fressinet
Artyom Timofeev
Plovdiv 2012 (5)

When I started my preparation for this game, I quickly concluded that my opponent's main weapon is the Grünfeld, which perfectly fits his active and dynamic style.

Immediately a recent interview with Matthew Sadler came to mind. He declared that one of the positive points of no longer being a professional chess player was that when he woke up in the morning he no longer had to ask himself what to play against the Grünfeld! To be honest, I ask myself that question before every tournament, and this time I had decided to be a bit lazier than normal and to follow the recommendations of Avrukh in his books *The Grünfeld Defence* 1 & 2 (Grandmaster Repertoire Volumes 8 & 9).

When I was asked to annotate one of my games from the championship at short notice, I considered my game against Timofeev to be the best choice. The only small problem was that on my way back from Plovdiv my air company had lost my suitcase and the book that was in it. Fortunately, the next day my suitcase arrived after all, so that I am now able to share with you a game with remarkable notes by Mr. Avrukh.

1.d4 ♘f6 2.c4 g6 3.♘f3 ♗g7 4.g3 c6 5.♗g2 d5

Artyom chooses the most solid system against the g3-Grünfeld.

6.b3!?
This is the move recommended by Boris Avrukh in his book. White tries to consolidate his centre.

The main line is 6.cxd5 cxd5, but White rarely obtains an opening advantage in this symmetrical structure.

6...dxc4
Normally Black castles before taking on c4. This move order adds some possibilities for Black, but most of the time Black is forced to transpose to the main line.

7.bxc4 c5

Black tries to tactically refute the white concept. As the move b3 has weakened the a1-h8 diagonal, Black tries to profit immediately.

8.♗b2 cxd4 9.♘xd4 ♕b6 10.♕b3 ♘fd7 11.0-0!
One of the points that are explained in the book. This tactical twist allows White not to protect the knight on d4.

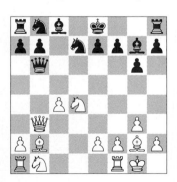

11...0-0
Now we have returned to the main variation.

After 11...♗xd4 Avrukh gives the following line, which seems to me to

Laurent Fressinet: 'Fortunately, the next day my suitcase arrived after all, so that I am now able to share with you a game with remarkable notes by Mr. Avrukh.'

be correct: 12.♕xb6 ♗xb6 13.♗xh8 f6 (Black tries to trap the bishop on h8 and threatens ...♗d4) 14.a4! ♔f7 15.a5 ♗d4 16.♖a3 ♘c5 (16...♔g8 17.♖d1 ♗c5 18.♖b3 ♘a6 19.♗h3 is more than excellent for White) 17. ♖d1 ♗e5 18.♖e3 ♘c6 19.♗xc6 bxc6 20.♖xe5 fxe5 21.♗xe5, and White has an extra pawn.

12.e3 ♘c6 13.♘c3

Avrukh gives two exclamation marks to this pawn sacrifice. Houdini even thinks that any other move already hands the advantage to Black.

13...♘a5
After this move I thought I was out of book, but it was only my memory playing tricks on me... So I started thinking on my own.

13...♘xd4 is the main line, but as is explained very well in the book, after 14.exd4 ♕xb3 15.axb3 ♗xd4 16.♖fd1

White has a lead in development that is at least sufficient compensation for the pawn. It should be noted that Black cannot defend the bishop with the natural 16...e5, as after 17.♖xd4! exd4 18.♘d5 White dominates.

14.♕c2!
It seemed to me during the game that this was the only move that could cause Black problems. It is also Avrukh's recommendation.

14...♘xc4
After 14...♘e5 15.♘d5 ♕d8 16.c5 ♘ac4 17.♖ab1 White has a slight advantage, according to Avrukh. Once again I agree with his assessment.

15.♘d5 ♕xb2 16.♘xe7+ ♔h8 17.♕xc4
After these tactical skirmishes White has regained the pawn and has a lead in development. It also has to be pointed out that the pawn on b7 will be a chronic weakness.

17...♛b6?
A novelty, according to the book, and a significant error!

The recommended move is 17...♞b6, and after 18.♕c5 Avrukh stops and concludes that White has a slight advantage. Black can continue with 18...♖e8, but after 19.♞d5 ♝g4 20.♖ab1 ♕xa2 21.♞xb6 axb6 22.♖xb6 White is going to win the pawn on b7 and has good winning chances.

18.♖fc1
During the game I was tempted by the interesting 18.♕d5!?, but it looked as if Black would hold after 18...♞f6 19.♞xc8 (better is 19.♕f3!, but I missed this move during the game: 19...♝g4 20.♕xb7 ♕xb7 21.♝xb7 ♖ae8 22.♞ec6, and Black is simply a pawn down) 19...♞xd5 20.♞xb6 ♞xb6 21.♝xb7 ♝xd4 22.exd4 ♖ad8 23.♖fd1 ♖d7 24.♝c6 ♖d6, and Black will probably win back the pawn on d4.

18...♝xd4 This looks very passive, but there is no good alternative. After 18...♕d8 19.♕b4 ♞e5 20.♖xc8 ♖xc8 21.♞xc8 ♖xc8 22.♕xb7 White wins a pawn.
19.♕xd4+ ♕xd4 20.exd4 ♖d8 21.♖c7

White seems to be totally dominating, but things are not that simple. He has to choose between different endgames with an extra pawn. It is clear that Black will suffer, but he has reasonable chances to save the half point.
21...♚g7 22.a4
Here 22.♝xb7! was less subtle than the move played, but probably more efficient: 22...♝xb7 23.♖xb7 ♞b6 24.♞c6 ♖d7 25.♖xd7 ♞xd7 26.♖b1, and Black's chances to save the draw look rather meagre.
22...a5 23.♖b1 The idea behind including the moves 22.a4 and 22...a5 was not to allow Black to install the

knight on b6, in view of the rook on b1.
23...♞f6 I had no choice; the pawn on b7 had to be taken now.

24.♝xb7 ♝xb7 25.♖bxb7 ♞e8 The only move. Black could not tolerate the two white rooks on the seventh rank.
26.♖d7 ♞d6 27.♖xd8 ♖xd8 28.♖c7 ♖b8 The right move. Black cannot remain passive and has to activate the rook. **29.♞c6**

29...♖b2?

This mistake is based on a calculating error. In the post-mortem Artyom and I concluded that the knight ending arising after 29...♖c8 30.♖xc8 ♘xc8 31.♘xa5 ♘b6 32.♔g2 ♔f6 33.♔f3 ♘xa4 34.♔e4 should be lost, as it is known that the assessment of a knight ending is often the same as that of a pawn ending (the same ending without the knights).

Probably, 29...♖b1+ was the best chance: 30.♔g2 ♖a1 31.♘d7 ♘f5 32. ♘xa5 ♖xa4 33.♘c6 ♖a2, and even though the draw is still far away, Black has succeeded in activating his pieces.

30.♘xa5

30...♘e4?

As always, a mistake never comes alone. It was still possible to defend a difficult endgame a pawn down after 30...♖b4 31.♘c6 ♖xa4 32.♖d7 ♘f5 (32...♘c8 33.♘e5 ♖a7 34.♖xa7 ♘xa7 35.♔f1 returns to the knight ending that is probably lost) 33.d5 ♖a1+ 34.♔g2 ♖a2, when compared to the note to 29...♖b1, Black has lost a tempo, which obviously will not make his defence any easier.

31.♘c4 ♖c2

It seems as if White has tied himself up, but the little tactical point

32.♘d6! allows him to untangle. Now 32...♖xc7 33.♘e8+ wins back the rook while keeping the two extra pawns.

And so Black resigned.

NOTES BY
Vladimir Malakhov

EO 36.14 – A34
Vladimir Malakhov
Artyom Timofeev
Plovdiv 2012 (7)

This game was played in Round 7, when both of us were on +3. In order to achieve our minimal goal – to qualify for the World Cup – we both needed to win at least one more game. So we were both in a fighting mood.

1.c4

Normally, if White is ready to go for some forced theoretical line, he starts with either 1.e4 or 1.d4. Other opening moves often mean that White wants to steer away from well-known lines and soon there will be some new position. But here the situation was different – against 1.c4 Artyom normally plays a sharp but slightly risky line, so at home I could prepare a certain position that I thought was quite likely to occur in the game (and did).

1...c5 2.♘f3 ♘f6 3.♘c3 d5 4. cxd5 ♘xd5 5.g3 ♘c6 6.♗g2 ♘c7

7.d3

Also interesting is 7.0-0, with the idea of a3, b4 without playing d2-d3, as Vladimir Kramnik played against Timofeev in the Russian champion-

ship Super Final in 2011. That game continued 7...e5 8.a3 ♗e7 9.b4 0-0 10. bxc5 ♗xc5 11.♗b2 ♖e8 12.♖c1 with a slight edge for White. But I went for another position.

7...e5 8.0-0 ♗e7 9.♘d2 ♗d7 10. ♘c4 f6 11.f4 b5 12.♘e3

12...♖c8?!

My opponent had already played this move several times, so I was expecting it, but in my opinion a safer way is 12...exf4, followed by 13...0-0, with an unclear position.

13.a4 b4 14.♘b5 exf4

15.♘c4!

This is the critical line I was aiming for. In the game Khairullin-Timofeev, Russian Cup Final 2010, White preferred 15.♖xf4 ♘xb5 16.axb5 ♘d4 17. ♖xa7 ♘xb5 18.♖a6 0-0 19.♘f5, with a slight edge, but I was sure that Artyom knew how to equalize here. Also the move I played is much sharper and much more interesting. This is not a novelty but a very rare continuation, first played in Lautier-Leko, Batumi 1999. White sacrifices a pawn, is later ready to give a second one, but has a very strong initiative for it. Houdini shows an advantage for White two pawns down, which means that Black's position is very dangerous.

15...fxg3

Another critical line is 15...♘xb5 16. axb5 ♘d4 17.♖xa7. Here Black has several possibilities, but everywhere White's initiative is strong.

For example: 17...♘xb5 18.♖b7 fxg3 19.♗f4! gxh2+ 20.♗xh2 0-0 21.♘b6, and White is better.

Leko, against Lautier, chose 17...♗g4?! 18.♖f2 0-0 19.b6 fxg3 20.hxg3 g5, and here instead of 21.♕f1?! White could have played 21.♗e3! ♘b5 22.♕a4 ♗d7 23.♕a6, with a huge advantage. After 17...fxg3 White has a choice – either to go for 18.b6 gxh2+ 19.♔h1 0-0 20.♗f4 ♗c6 21.♖f2 (or 21.b7) with a very unclear position, or to play 18. ♗f4!? gxh2+ 19.♗xh2 ♘xb5, which leads to the same position as after 17... ♘xb5.

16.♘bd6+

16...♗xd6!?

This is a novelty. In 2002 Dominguez, in a game against another Cuban player, preferred 16...♔f8, and after 17.hxg3?! ♖b8 18.♗e3 ♘e6 he got an acceptable position. Instead, White should have played 17.♗f4! gxh2+

18.♗xh2 ♖b8 19.e3, with very strong compensation.

It is very uneasy to play this kind of position with black, so after some deep thought my opponent decided to sacrifice an exchange for just one pawn, but put his king on e7 to give his second rook a chance to come into play.

17.♘xd6+ ♔e7

18.♘xc8+

I was also thinking about 18.♗f4!, which was really very interesting. Artyom had planned 18...♘e6 19. ♗xg3 h5, but after 20.♘xc8+ ♕xc8 21.♖c1 h4 22.♗f2 h3 23.♗e4 ♖h5 24.e3 ♖g5+ 25.♗g3 White is clearly better. I was worried about 18...gxh2+ 19.♗xh2 ♘e6 20.e3 ♕b6. But after 21.♕h5 ♖g5 22.♗f4! h6 23.♘c4 ♕b7 24.♗d6+ ♔d8 25.♗xc5 or 21...♖cf8 22.♘c4 White's attack is very strong, so I should probably have gone for it. After the move I played White has a material advantage, but Black completes his development and has some compensation for the material deficit.

18...♕xc8 19.hxg3

19...♘d4

	Plovdiv 2012				TPR
1	Dmitry Jakovenko	2729	RUS	8½	2832
2	Laurent Fressinet	2693	FRA	8	2800
3	Vladimir Malakhov	2705	RUS	8	2787
4	Dmitry Andreikin	2689	RUS	8	2786
5	Ernesto Inarkiev	2695	RUS	8	2784
6	Maxim Matlakov	2632	RUS	8	2778
7	Victor Bologan	2687	MDA	8	2768
8	Francisco Vallejo	2693	ESP	8	2765
9	Yury Kryvoruchko	2666	UKR	8	2761
10	Sergey Azarov	2667	BLR	8	2759
11	Evgeny Najer	2640	RUS	8	2756
12	Vladimir Akopian	2684	ARM	8	2754
13	Andrey Volokitin	2695	UKR	8	2745
14	Jan Smeets	2610	NED	8	2685
15	Gawain Jones	2635	ENG	7½	2760
16	Nikita Vitiugov	2709	RUS	7½	2751
17	Etienne Bacrot	2706	FRA	7½	2748
18	Alexey Dreev	2698	RUS	7½	2736
19	Denis Khismatullin	2656	RUS	7½	2734
20	Mikhail Kobalia	2666	RUS	7½	2734
21	Vasif Durarbeyli	2543	AZE	7½	2729
22	Alexander Riazantsev	2710	RUS	7½	2728
23	Baadur Jobava	2706	GEO	7½	2725
24	Ferenc Berkes	2682	HUN	7½	2716
25	Markus Ragger	2654	AUT	7½	2714
26	Csaba Balogh	2664	HUN	7½	2714
27	Daniel Fridman	2653	GER	7½	2709
28	Liviu-Dieter Nisipeanu	2643	ROU	7½	2706
29	Ivan Sokolov	2653	NED	7½	2705
30	Kiril Georgiev	2671	BUL	7½	2703
31	Gabriel Sargissian	2674	ARM	7½	2702
32	Ivan Ivanisevic	2645	SRB	7½	2698
33	Sanan Sjugirov	2610	RUS	7½	2697
34	Igor Khenkin	2632	GER	7½	2695
35	Zahar Efimenko	2695	UKR	7½	2664
36	Sergey Grigoriants	2561	RUS	7½	2647
37	Yury Kuzubov	2615	UKR	7	2727
38	Fabiano Caruana	2767	ITA	7	2720
39	Arkadij Naiditsch	2702	GER	7	2710
40	Hrant Melkumyan	2628	ARM	7	2700
	348 players, 11 rounds				

The right idea, to exchange the light-squared bishops. After 19...♘e6 20. ♗e3 ♕c7 21.♗f2 ♖d8 22.♖c1 Black has some problems with the c5-pawn, and 22...♘cd4 is already met by 23.e3!.

20.♗e3 ♘ce6 21.♖c1 ♖d8!

Worse was 21...♕c7 22.♗xd4 ♘xd4 23.e3 ♘e6 24.♕g4, and White is clearly better, as well as after 21...♕a6 22.♗xd4 cxd4 23.♖c4! ♕d6 24.♕e1 a5 25.♖f5.

22.♖c4!

It is very important for White to exchange rooks here, otherwise Black may get some initiative with the combined ♕+♖+♘. The move I played helps to achieve this goal after 22...♗c6, the move Black has to play, because White threatens 23.♗d4. The immediate 22.♗xd4?! was not good because of 22...♘xd4, and now 23.e3 is not possible due to 23...♗g4.

22...♗c6 23.♗xd4 ♖xd4

The interesting line 23...♘xd4 24. ♖xc5 ♕g4 didn't work – after 25. ♗xc6 ♘xe2+ (or 25...♘xc6 26.♕e1) 26.♔f2 ♕d4+ 27.♔g2 White wins.

24.♖xd4

A knack for European championships. Following second places in Budva and Istanbul, Vladimir Malakhov took third place in Plovdiv.

24...♗xg2?!

Now White keeps the rook on the 4th rank, where it is perfectly positioned. Better was 24...♘xd4 25.♗xc6 (after 25.e3 ♗xg2 26.♔xg2 ♘e6, followed by ...♘g5, Black should have enough counterplay) 25...♕xc6 26.e3 ♘e6, which would have offered better saving chances, for example: 27.d4 ♕e4! 28.dxc5 ♕xe3+ 29.♔h2 ♕xc5. After the text-move Black's position is difficult.

25.♖c4! ♗xf1 26.♕xf1 ♕c6 27.♕f5 ♕xa4 28.♖e4 ♕c6 29.♕xh7 ♔f7 30.♕h5+ ♔f8

In case of 30...♔g8, avoiding the idea ♕h8-b8, White could try 31.g4!, threatening 32.g5, and Black has to go to f8 anyway.

31.♔f2!? Maybe even better was the immediate 31.♕h8+ ♔f7 32.♕b8 ♕d7 33.♕a8 ♘g5 34.♖c4, and White must win eventually.

31...a5?! He had probably missed my next move, which leads to a queen ending in which White is a pawn up and should be winning.

Better was 31...♘g5, but here, after 32.♕h8+ ♔f7 33.♖c4, followed by 34.♕b8, Black has little chance to save himself.

32.♖xe6 ♕xe6 33.♕xc5+ ♔f7

34.♕xa5 ♕b3 35.♕a7+ ♔g6 36.♕d4 ♔h6 37.g4

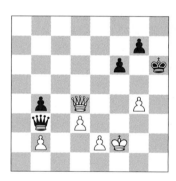

37...♔g6?

This final mistake leads to an immediate win for White. The only way was 37...♔h7, and here something like 38.♔e3 ♔h6 39.♕f4+ ♔h7 40.♕e4+ ♔h8 (40...♔h6 41.♕f5 and game over) 41.♕d4 ♔h7 42.♔d2 ♔g6 43.♕e4+ ♔h6 (after 43...♔g5 44.♔e3! White wins) 44.♕f4+ ♔h7 45.♕f5+ ♔g8 46.♔c1 ♕a4 47.♕e6+ ♔f8 48.♕c4, and step by step White must win this endgame.

38.♕e4+

38...♔f7 is impossible due to 39.♕c4+, and after 38...♔h6 39.♕f5 g6 (or 39...♕f7 40.g5+ ♔h5 41.g6+) 40.♕xf6 White wins a second pawn. So Black resigned. ∎

Saturday Night Fever

About ten years ago I was asked by one of the leading South African women players whether I could recommend a few books to study. In return, I asked what tomes she already possessed. She answered, to my surprise, that her father had an ample library of around 500 volumes at home. I then suggested, perhaps a little undiplomatically, that she would benefit by reading some of them. My advice obviously didn't go down well, because that was almost the last I heard from her...

Shortcuts undoubtedly have considerable use, but there is a limit to what one can achieve without hard labour. Malcolm Gladwell, in his superb book *Outliers: The Story of Success*, refers to the 10,000 hours of practice necessary to achieve expertise in almost anything. One can quibble about the precise figure (and I do) but, nevertheless, his general point remains valid. In a difficult discipline, like chess, you have to immerse yourself fully if you wish to reach the top. One can accelerate the acquisition of knowledge with judiciousness, but one cannot circumvent this process.

Looking back on my own career, I can identify a number of omissions, by far the most serious of which was never really acquiring the habit of studying systematically, which was probably due to the absence of a coach in my formative years. However, my parents certainly got at least one thing right: I never wanted for opportunities to compete. By my early teens, I was regularly playing around 150+ nationally rated games per year – more than anyone else in the north of England, and far more than I have ever done as a professional – all while still attending school (no wonder I did so badly). There were many club and county games, but probably the biggest proportion of the total came from weekend tournaments. Yes, that most grubby, sweaty, smelly form of chess unquestionably played a key part in my development.

Digressing slightly, but still on the subject of personal hygiene (apparently a matter of great topicality for the European Chess Union), I am reminded of a story told to me a few years ago by the Scottish journalist John Henderson. He was telephoned by a British-based GM of Croatian origin who asked whether he could stay at his pad over the Friday and Saturday. John kindly agreed and duly provided his guest with a sleeping bag when he arrived. The next morning John entered the living room early to wake his companion, but was surprised when his disheveled guest immediately sprang forth from his sleeping bag, still wearing a crumpled suit...

As Garry Kasparov relates in his latest autobiography, the patriarch of Soviet chess, Mikhail Botvinnik, was vehemently opposed to even regular Swiss tournaments on stern ideological grounds. Goodness knows what he thought about the humble weekender, with its grueling schedule and six games crammed into two and a bit days. It is about as far removed from the maestro's concept of the proper chess, with soporific time-controls, adjournment-days, free days etc., as one can imagine. Mind you, Botvinnik was a communist, so he obviously wasn't right about everything. Perhaps he also underestimated the value of learning by experience.

Indeed, the plebeian weekend format has, over the years, provided a great number of players, at least in my own country, with a very useful rudimentary education. It is hardly surprising that this should be so: the vast majority of people are amateurs and, with obligations such as work or school, they simply don't have sufficient time to devote themselves totally to the game. Whatever time they do have available must be utilized to the full. Concentrating so much practice into so few hours is clearly not ideal, but it is effective.

The heyday of the weekender was, of course, the Fischer-boom years. Entries for the Islington Congress – a leading tournament at the time – jumped from over 500 (in itself a very respectable figure) in 1971, to over 1,200 the following year. This pattern of record participation was repeated throughout the country in the immediate aftermath of Reykjavik; the numbers would later drop back, although not to the pre-Fischer levels, as the initial tidal wave of enthusiasm receded. New tournaments also came into existence, which meant, for the most part, your writer didn't have to venture far from home, as competitions in Bolton, Blackpool, Manchester, Chorley, Rochdale etc. were all in easy striking distance.

As an aspiring junior, the most beneficial aspect of the weekend circuit was regularly encountering strong opposition, who I would not necessarily meet in my local leagues. This generally meant guys with 2200+ Elo, but occasionally I would run across someone considerably stronger. After scything down three opponents at the 1976 Charlton Open, I found myself, having just turned 11 years old, being down-floated to Tony Miles! Indeed Britain's first Grandmaster was a regular in these dirty events until he graduated on to better things a year or two after obtaining his title. His tenacity, stamina and sheer determination to grind down opposition were, however, honed in this harsh, Darwinian environment, which contrasted sharply to the consensual, pacific ethos that prevailed in one or two places that I could mention.

While it is true the weekend circuit never offered riches, the 700 pounds first prize in the National Bank of Dubai Open in the late 70s (worth several times that figure in today's money), for instance, was sufficient to attract a strong international entry. Naturally most tournaments offered less, but the most successful practitioner of the year could expect to collect a couple of thousand pounds (not forgetting a gallon of whisky) as winner of the Cutty Sark Grand Prix.

Alas, today's prizes have not kept pace with the ravages of inflation. Even a fairly major event, like the recently completed Blackpool Congress, offered just a modest 800 pounds victor's purse. Why there has been a relative decline is a matter of conjecture. Not all countries have a

similar chess structure: in Germany, for example, the Bundesliga provides an arguably superior alternative, but in mine, weekenders are a barometer of our nation's chess health.

Entire opening systems have – if not exactly been born – flourished in the environment where opening preparation is close to impossible. The most obvious example is the eponymous Grand Prix Attack. The attractions of this simple line, which has claimed literally thousands of victims over the years, are obvious. There is no necessity to memorise masses of Open Sicilian theory – just two or three basic ideas will suffice. And for those snobs who imagine that such crude and primitive ideas cannot work at a higher level – a quick look at Short-Gelfand, Brussels Candidates' Match (3) 1991, Short-Oll, Tallinn 1997 and Short-Hou Yifan, Gibraltar 2012, ought to be sufficient to dispel such illusions. It may not provide a complete repertoire, but it is definitely a very potent supplementary weapon.

Since becoming a professional three decades ago and dieting on far more lucrative round-robins, matches etc., I had almost forgotten what such events were like, but in the last couple of years I have had the pleasure of participating in the Rolls-Royce of weekenders – the Bunratty Chess Festival in the west of Ireland. The luxurious rooms and spa facilities at the Bunratty Castle Hotel are a far cry from the grim conditions of my youth, as in-

deed are the appearance fees – without which I wouldn't be playing, of course. It goes without saying that Irish hospitality is rightly famous and it is no wonder that Peter Svidler has been tempted to the green extremity of Europe more than once in the past. Nevertheless certain aspects of the format – such as that desperate feeling of 'why am I here?' during that third game on Saturday night – haven't changed at all. In 2011 I made the serious mistake of playing two lengthy endgames against Adam Hunt and Sam Collins before receiving a deadly triple-whammy to my sanity by being paired black against Gawain Jones – who by now is acquiring a deserved international reputation as a formidable opponent. By this time my brain had already turned into a blancmange – and that was even before I had started on the Guinness. Try as I might, I could not recall more than two or three theoretical moves of a line I had studied in immense depth just a couple of months previously and so I found myself trapped into playing something which I well knew to be inferior. There is only one thing worse than being wiped out quickly and that is losing slowly and painfully. As Sod's Law would have it, I somehow survived into a passive rook and pawn endgame before eventually, after what seemed like an eternity, being put out of my squalid misery. This year I took a more pragmatic approach to the ordeal that is Saturday: I made a conscious decision to play fast and badly. It worked a treat: I won all three games. ∎

> 'Yes, that most grubby, sweaty, smelly form of chess unquestionably played a key part in my development.'

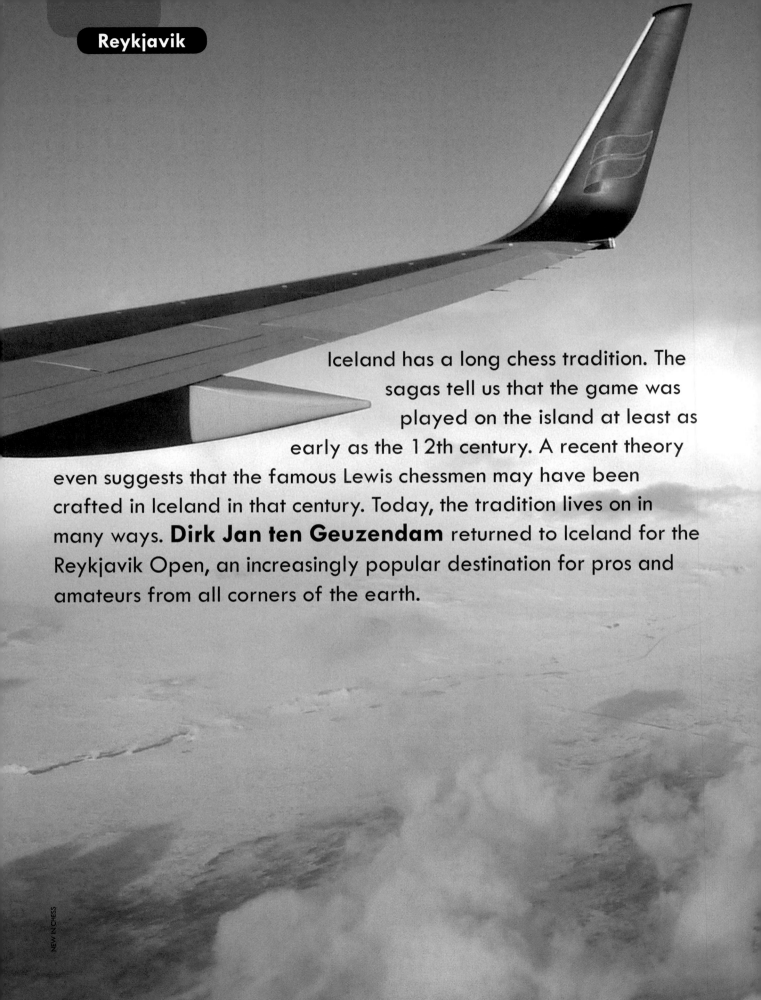

Iceland has a long chess tradition. The sagas tell us that the game was played on the island at least as early as the 12th century. A recent theory even suggests that the famous Lewis chessmen may have been crafted in Iceland in that century. Today, the tradition lives on in many ways. **Dirk Jan ten Geuzendam** returned to Iceland for the Reykjavik Open, an increasingly popular destination for pros and amateurs from all corners of the earth.

Chess City Reykjavik

Chess seems to be highly respected in Iceland, Gawain Jones noted. At least the English grandmaster could not remember ever having had the response he got when he asked for a chess set in a Reykjavik sports bar. The girl behind the bar just nodded and handed him four different types of chess sets to choose from. To be honest, her reaction no longer came as a real surprise for Jones, as he also played in the Reykjavik Open last year, when the tournament was hosted in a big conference room in City Hall. With a smile he remembered that the pond in front of the hall was frozen over, offering the participants an additional route to be in time for their games.

With a steady increase of participants, from 110 in 2010 and 166 in 2011 to 198 this time, the City Hall had become too small, so the Reykjavik Open moved to Harpa, the stunning new concert hall near the harbour. Harpa can be seen as a symbol of the economic crisis that hit Iceland in the course of 2008. When I was in Reykjavik in February of that year, my hosts would proudly point at the emerging contours of a building that was still under construction. It was going to be one of the most spectacular music halls in Europe and next to it a 400-room hotel would arise, a World Trade Centre, luxury apartments and the new headquarters of Landsbanki, one of the three national banks that collapsed in the crisis together with the Glitnir and Kaupthing banks.

NEW IN CHESS

Harpa, an architectural marvel of steel, glass and light, is the new home of the Reykjavik Open.

The future in action. Hilmir Heimisson is about to defeat Nansy Davidsdottir in the final of a junior blitz tournament. Vignir Stefansson follows the game with crossed arms.

Most of these construction dreams inevitably went up in smoke, but the Icelandic government decided to fully fund the completion of the half-built concert hall, which was festively opened in December 2009. Both from the outside and the inside Harpa is a breathtaking sight, and it is easy to understand that the total cost amounted to 164 million euros. Still, even with that sum the original plans could not be fully realized. If you look carefully, you will see small imperfections. A sign that kept intriguing me was one indicating a toilet for the disabled that pointed down a steep staircase without an elevator in sight.

Harpa contains several halls, the biggest one with a capacity of 1800 seats. The Reykjavik Open took place on the ground floor in a large open space close to an excellent restaurant and cafeteria. Through the windows the participants had an extensive view of the harbour and the mountains in the distance. Less welcome was the fact that the open space allowed sounds from elsewhere in the building to be heard. Especially activities involving large groups of kids or dance music disturbed the players. Faced by this problem, there was lit-

tle the organizers could do but offer earplugs this time. For next time they have promised quieter conditions.

According to Gunnar Bjornsson, the president of the Icelandic Chess Federation, the financial crisis also had a good side. There is less work, people have less money and accordingly travel less. That sounds bleak, but there is a clear indication that the 'back-to-basics' attitude that came with the recession has resulted in more and more people discovering or rediscovering chess.

Although he already was involved in chess organizing for many years, Bjornsson's presidency of the federation is in a way also connected to the crisis. Working in the risk department of Landsbanki he saw the chaos and panic from close by. Bjornsson remembers a terrible time, when many of his colleagues lost their jobs and he and other colleagues were only working to deal with the crisis. He is still at Landsbanki, but in 2009, partly because of a decrease in work at the bank, he was allowed to spend 60 per cent of his time working as President of the federation.

Bjornsson's estimate is that half of

his time as President is devoted to the Reykjavik Open. His ambition is to turn the event into one of the major Opens in the world and thus create an ideal platform for Icelandic talents to develop. With the 2012 edition he showed that considerable progress has been made. More than 20 GMs took part and the field was composed of a wide variety of nationalities. And the youngest Icelandic hopes competed as well, of course. Maybe one day soon you will hear more from the following talents: Vignir Stefansson (9), Hilmir Heimisson (10) or Nansy Davidsdottir (10).

Open tournaments are said to be distinctly different from closed tournaments and they certainly are. To begin with, it is perfectly understandable why the junior talents just mentioned, and strong amateurs from abroad for that matter, jump at such a wonderful opportunity to gain experience. The issue becomes more complicated if you look at the GMs who are trying to make a living out of chess and cannot count on support from a sponsor or their federation, such as the Asian participants. With no starting fees and at best conditions such as hotel and flight, they take a considerable risk. First prize in Reykjavik was €5,000, not bad for 9 days of work, but the second prize, €1,500, was already considerably less attractive. As it was, this second prize was won by nobody, because of a massive tie for second, which is not unusual in Opens. Seven players split the prices for places 2 to 8 between them, each of them going home with €500.

To get a better idea of the economy of open tournaments, it would be interesting to know what their net earnings were. Life in Iceland these days is considerably less expensive than it was some years ago, but calling it cheap would still be beside the truth. Sitting in a shuttle bus between the city centre and my hotel, I listened in amusement to the following exchange of yells between the bus driver, a man with comical talents, and a group of Americans he welcomed on board: 'Did you have a good time?' 'Yes!!' 'Was it expensive?' 'Yes!!' 'Was it worth it?' 'Yes!!'

Because of these modest earnings and the realistic chance that you don't make any money, Opens seem to see more incidents and manifestations of stress. The Reykjavik Open was a smooth event that passed in a friendly atmosphere, but still there was clearly more friction than tends to crop up in closed tournaments. There is less at stake, and exactly for that reason it feels like so much more. One of the disagreements is described by Gawain Jones in the notes to his eventful game against Stelios Halkias. The Englishman asked his opponent to abide by the rules and write down his moves only after he had made them, a request that wasn't appreciated by the Greek GM. In his defence, Halkias pointed out that writing down his moves before making them is an old habit of his. He acknowledged that he sinned against the new rules but also stressed that Jones had not cared about his old habit during their game at the European Team Championships in Porto Carras. There the English GM had had a winning position (and won), whereas here his position was highly problematic. It sounds as if both players had a point, but it seems safe to say that they both were under considerable pressure. The winner would still be in the running for a top spot, whereas the loser would almost certainly have spoiled his tournament.

Irritation and frustration also played a part in the dispute between Hedinn Steingrimsson and Kore Akshayraj. The Icelandic champion quickly gained a reputation for regularly trying to pull the board closer to himself, apparently to have a better view of what was going on. This was not appreciated by all his opponents, and while the Icelander was pulling at the board, they were often trying to keep it in the middle of the table. Akshayraj, an Indian IM who would miss a GM-norm by losing his last-round game against Gawain Jones, objected

to Steingrimsson's pulling at the board in Round 5 and told the arbiter. Steingrimsson in his turn accused the Indian of not writing down his moves, and in the deteriorating atmosphere Akshayraj was even inadvertently kicked against his legs. Still, it was Steingrimsson who was affected most by the exchange of complaints.

Steingrimsson-Akshayraj
position after 50...♗e7

With an exchange and a pawn up, even if it's a doubled one, White should be winning without too many problems. But there is one pitfall he should beware of... **51.♖b7?** And White falls for it. It's almost comical how much material White loses immediately with this oversight. **51...♗xh4+!** A rude awakening. In four consecutive moves Black bags three pawns and an exchange. **52.♔xh4 ♕xf4+ 53.♔h3 ♕xf3+ 54.♔h2 ♕xb7** and being two healthy pawns up Black won easily, even though Steingrimsson chose to protract his suffering till move 73.

The first prize of €5,000 was won by top-seed Fabiano Caruana. It rarely happens that a top-10 player participates in an Open. It's a common and often-heard opinion from players who seldom if ever get invited to closed events that colleagues spoiled in that safe world would have a hard time in the jungle of the Opens. Here you cannot think that not losing is more important than winning, because winning is imperative, as only one big prize waits at the end. Still, this grumbling should not be interpreted as an invitation for top players to play

Between games the cafetaria and restaurant in the huge foyer of Harpa were perfect spots to have a drink or a meal.

Opens. After all, who wants to have a big shark in the pond if there is too little food to begin with? It's the other way around. What they are really trying to say is that they, too, would stand a good chance in the protected environment of a closed tournament.

Perhaps Caruana's participation wasn't greeted with enthusiasm by the other GMs in Reykjavik, but no one vented his (or her) unhappiness publicly. Funnily enough, criticism of his presence came from a completely different corner. Seeing that Caruana was threatening his number 6 position in the world rankings after a 4/4 start against mainly weaker opponents (they were rated 2102, 2346, 2461 and 2611 respectively, which earned him 5.8 rating points), Hikaru Nakamura tweeted: 'After seeing people picking up rating points off of beating weaker players, I am convinced chess ratings should be weighted like in tennis.' Nakamura, one of very few top players who occasionally play in Opens, need not have worried: in his last five games Caruana 'only' scored 3½ out of 5, which against an average opposition of 2602 meant a loss of 0.4 points. So in total he gathered 5.4 rating points, which seems a just reward for an outstanding result that most top-10 players would be pleased with.

Caruana didn't want to enter into a debate about Nakamura's tweet. 'It doesn't bother me. I don't think there is any reason that a player would come here to try to make points. Of course it's not easy at all. You have to play some very strong players and you have to make a lot of points. A tournament like this can be just as hard as a tournament like Wijk aan Zee or Reggio Emilia. I make my own decisions and of course everyone can have their own opinion, but I am not bothered by that.' His main reason, Caruana stressed, is that currently he wants to play as much as possible, which also explained his participation in the tough Aeroflot Open, where he also picked up four rating points. 'I'm trying to be active. I think it's very important to play as much as possible actually, to keep fresh. If you don't play for

a long time it's possible that you lose some strength, at least that's my feeling. Many top players play more sporadically, one tournament every two months, but for me I am quite happy playing as much as I can.'

Caruana struck on the dreaded 'double-round' day, when both Rounds 6 and 7 were played. This double round so late in the tournament was the only criticism Gawain Jones had, and it is hard to argue with his reasoning: 'This I really dislike, because those are actually important rounds for the tournament. If you have to have a double round – and it's much better, of course, if there is none at all – then Rounds 2 and 3 or something are far better, when there are still some mismatches and it doesn't matter if you have one loss; you can still get back into it.'

Caruana entered 'Bloody Sunday', which started with Round 6 at 9.30(!), in the morning and continued with Round 7 at 4.30 in the afternoon, trailing Cheparinov and Sokolov by half a point. He emerged half a point ahead of Avrukh and Sokolov. His two wins differed considerably. Against Icelandic IM Bragi Thorfinnsson he had to

work hard to eke out a win, while his win against rival Cheparinov was a smooth affair, a model game that any Grünfeld player should study.

Two draws in the final rounds sufficed for sole tournament victory, but these games, too, were hard-fought. Playing white against Ivan Sokolov, Caruana was treated to one of the Spanish specialties of the Dutch grandmaster and was slightly worse for most of the game. In the last round he was even lost. Hou Yifan achieved a very promising position, but failed to find the decisive blow.

Hou Yifan-Caruana
position after 40...♗b7

With strong and deep play Hou Yifan has driven the tournament leader with his back against the wall. Is White winning? No one dared to say for sure, particularly not at the end of the last game of a tough event. **41.♘xf7?** Tempting, but this move actually throws away the win. White could win with the very precise sequence 41.♘ac4 ♘xe4 42.d7 ♖d8 43.♘a5 ♗d5 44.♖d3 ♘f6 45.♖xd5 ♘xd5 46.♘b7, and the extra white knight (against a pawn) should carry the day. After the text-move the position quickly petered out to a draw. **41...♔xf7 42.♖f3+ ♔e6 43.♘b5 ♖b8 44.♖xf2 ♗xe4 45.♖e2 ♖xb5 46.♖xe4+ ♔xd6 47.♔g3 ♔d5** Draw.

Hou Yifan was one of the attractions of the Reykjavik Open. The Women's World Champion was not too happy about her play in the earlier rounds, but felt that she started to play better towards the end. After she had

Gunnar Bjornsson, the President of the Icelandic Chess Federation, looks justifiedly happy with Fabiano Caruana's superb victory.

NEW IN CHESS

disposed of GMs Hannes Stefansson and Vladimir Baklan in Rounds 7 and 8 she came close to claiming sole first place in the final encounter with Caruana and causing a new sensation after her result in Gibraltar.

As always, Hou Yifan let modesty prevail. Typical was her first reaction after she had ground down Baklan with the black pieces. Of course she was pleased with her win, but she immediately stressed that she had been lucky, as he could have saved the game with 37.♕a5.

Luck certainly plays a role in chess, but should you always call it luck if you keep looking for your chances and strike when the opportunity appears? Stefansson also had a defensible position, but it was slightly unpleasant too and finally he slipped up.

Hou Yifan (with flowers!) at the grave of her idol Bobby Fischer.

Hou Yifan-Stefansson
position after 30...♗e6

White has been exerting pressure for most of the game, but Hou Yifan seems to be looking in vain for a way to turn the pressure into something tangible. **31.♘f6+ ♔f8 32.♘h7+ ♔g8 33.♘f6+** First a repetition to gain some time. **33...♔f8 34.♖c5 ♘f5** With 34...♕d1+ 35.♔h2 ♕d2 36.♕xd2 ♖xd2 Black could have forced an endgame that should have been a draw. **35.♘h7+ ♔g8 36.♘f6+ ♔f8 37.♘d5!** After another repetition Hou Yifan hits on the right idea. Black has to tread very carefully now. **37...♔g8** Better was 37...♘e7 38.♘xe7 ♔xe7 39.♖c7+ ♖d7 40.♖xd7+ ♔xd7 41.♕e3, and although White's position is more pleasant to play, Black has good drawing chances. **38.♖c6**

38...♕b8? A very unfortunate square for the queen, as will soon become clear. Black could have fought on with 38...♕f8 39.♘f6+ ♔h8 40.♘xh5+ ♘d4 41.♘f4, although White obviously has excellent winning chances here. **39.♘f6+ ♔f8 40.♖xe6!** And Black resigned. After 40...fxe6, he can ward off the first attack on his queen, 41.♘d7+, with 41... ♖xd7, but not the second, 42.♕h8+, and the black queen is caught.

Fiske and Fischer

Many of the participants used the opportunity to do some sightseeing. A popular excursion was the Golden Circle tour, which not only included natural marvels such as geysers, but also a visit to Bobby Fischer's grave. For those interested in the 1972 match between Spassky and Fischer there was a small exhibition in the National Museum celebrating its 40th anniversary. Gudmundur Thorarinsson, the

organizer of the 1972 match, told me that he remains amazed how many foreign journalists still come to his house every year to talk about the match. He understands their fascination with the Match of the Century, but also tries to explain to them that it has taken on such mythical proportions (it's not for nothing that he has started to call it the 'Match of All Time') that he no longer has much to say about it. 'It's like children, they grow up and lead an independent life. The match is 40 years old and can take care of itself!'

Unfortunately, most of the participants were less familiar with another American who did a lot for Icelandic chess. Daniel Willard Fiske (1831-1904) was one of the organizers of the First American Congress in 1857 and a good friend of Paul Morphy's, Fischer's great predecessor. In 1868 he was named university librarian and Professor at Cornell University in Ithaca, New York. One of his passions was Icelandic language and culture. Fiske made many donations to Iceland and is fondly remembered on the small island of Grimsey, a chess-loving community, where he regularly sent supplies, including chess sets. One year after his death, his monumental study *Chess in Iceland* appeared. In his will he donated his chess library to the National Library of Iceland.

On the day after the last round I had the privilege of visiting the collection together with Einar Einarsson and Helgi Olafsson, two of the members of the RJF Committee that had worked to free Bobby Fischer from a Japanese detention centre. Compared to other famous collections, Fiske's library is modest in size, about 1500 volumes, but there is more than enough compensation in its quality. Most of the 19th century classics are there in excellent condition, and beautifully bound runs of the major chess magazines adorn the shelves. From the older treasures, an early Damiano can be mentioned, a Lolli with notes by the author and Allen's *Life of Philidor* with a dedication to Fiske by the author.

Einar and Helgi also took me to Fischer's grave near Selfoss. Spending time with two men who had known Fischer so well automatically resulted in several 'Bobby stories' that I had not heard before. Fortunately, Helgi has written down his memories of the American champion in his book *Bobby Fischer Comes Home*. Einar may follow his example. From the ease with which he treated me to anecdotes this should also be a book to look forward to. For instance, when I proudly told him that I had taken a small glass of cod liver oil from the hotel's breakfast buffet, he immediately explained that this had not

been good or strong enough for Bobby. He preferred shark liver oil! And when on another occasion we were talking about Fischer's complicated attitude towards other people, Einar remembered how shortly after his arrival in Iceland he had helped him find a cleaning lady. Einar knew a woman working for a friend of his and had recommended her to Fischer, saying she was a woman 'who always smiled'. On the first day she came to work, Einar received an angry phone call from Fischer, who told him that she didn't smile at all! He was right. The 'smiling' woman had had no time herself and had sent her sister. The problem was solved when she went herself the next time.

For Fabiano Caruana it felt special to play in the country where Bobby Fischer had found his last resting place. 'He is not someone I am trying to copy or anything, but I like to think I am following in his footsteps in some way. Of course, he was a player you have to look up to and he has achieved maybe more than any other player. Until I was 12, I played in all American tournaments and in a way he was always there. He's a player I have studied quite a lot. I would say that he and Kasparov were probably my two favourite players. When I started studying chess seriously, when I was twelve, I bought *My 60 Memora-*

ble Games and went through it almost completely. And I still have it.'

Hou Yifan said that one of the reasons she had accepted the invitation to play in Iceland was 'because it's the place of my idol Bobby Fischer. Whatever he played, the opening, the middlegame or the endgame, he was very strong. I don't know what exactly I learned from him, but I read *My 60 Memorable Games*, and played through most of the games.' Her favourite Fischer game was not in the original *M60MG*, but in the appendix of the edition she read. It was the seventh game from his 1971 Candidates' Final match against Petrosian in Buenos Aires, where Fischer gave up his strong knight with 22.♘xd7! to reach a favourable endgame and decided the game in his favour as early as move 34.

Hou Yifan took part in the excursion that included a visit to Fischer's grave. Standing at the grave she realized she didn't have any flowers and asked one of the organizers if they could go and buy flowers somewhere. After some searching they found a flower shop and after she had made her choice the organizer took out his wallet to pay for them. Hou Yifan was quick to stop him from doing so. There was no way that someone else was going to pay for this bouquet. These flowers for Bobby Fischer were from *her* and her alone.

GI 4.1 – D85
Ivan Cheparinov
Fabiano Caruana
Reykjavik 2012 (7)

This was the second game of the sixth day. In the morning game I had won a difficult rook ending to move into shared first place, and I only had a few hours rest before facing one of my toughest competitors in the tournament, Ivan Cheparinov. I think we both realized the result of this game would probably decide the eventual tournament winner.

1.d4 ♞f6 2.c4 g6 3.♞c3 d5 4. cxd5 ♞xd5 5.e4 ♞xc3 6.bxc3 ♝g7 7.♝b5+

A big surprise. I was expecting Ivan to test me in the principled 7.♝c4 variation.

7...c6 8.♝a4 0-0 9.♞e2 c5 10.0-0 ♞c6 11.♝e3 ♞a5

I didn't know much, but I did remember that this is some sort of theory, and all Black's moves seem pretty logical. The knight is heading for the c4 square.

12.dxc5

A rare move, and probably not one which will lead to a white advantage, but it does achieve double-edged play, with chances to gain the upper hand if Black plays inaccurately.

12...♛c7

I felt like keeping the queens on the board.

The alternative is 12...♞c4 13.♛xd8

♜xd8 14.♝g5 ♞d7 15.♝b3 ♞a5, which gave Black very nice results in practice, but perhaps White has some slight pull after 16.♜fd1 ♚f8 17.♞d4 ♜ac8 18.♝e3, since it isn't easy to regain the c5-pawn.

13.♝b3

After 13.♞f4 e6 14.♞d3 b6!, Black gets very strong compensation for the pawn. The bishop will come to a6, the knight to c4, and Black's activity will be hard to contain.

13...♝g4

Provoking f3 before withdrawing the bishop to d7 seems like a useful idea. In many lines it's helpful that c5 will hang with check.

14.f3 ♝d7

15.♛b1?!

A strange-looking move, after which the initiative passes to Black.

However, White had no way to play for an advantage. In case of the natural 15.♜c1, Black can respond 15... ♜fd8 16.♛e1 ♞xb3 17.axb3 a5!, with ...a4 coming next. The bishop pair and White's vulnerable pawns provide sufficient compensation.

15...e6 16.♜d1 ♜fd8 17.♚h1 ♝e8

Black's play is simple and logical.

White has no targets for attack, so I just secure my position and prepare to round up the c5-pawn with ...♝f8 and ...♝xc5.

Also possible was 17...♝b5 18.♞d4 ♛xc5, but it leads to drawish positions after 19.♛c1 ♞xb3 20.axb3 ♝e8 21.♞f5 ♛xc3 22.♞xg7 ♜xd1+ 23.♛xd1 ♛xe3 24.♞xe8 ♜xe8 25.♛d7 ♜b8 26.♛c7, regaining the pawn with an equal game.

18.♛b2?!

The computer's preference, but during the game it seemed dubious to me.

I was expecting the natural 18.♛c2 ♝f8 19.♜xd8 ♜xd8 20.♜d1, and felt the position was close to equal: 20... ♜xd1+ 21.♛xd1 ♝xc5 22.♝xc5 ♛xc5 23.♛d8 ♚f8 24.♝a4 ♞c6 25. ♝xc6 ♛xc6, with some small pull for Black, but White should be able to hold.

A radical solution I hadn't even noticed during the game is 18.♜d4!? ♝f8 (I'd rather avoid 18...♝xd4 19. cxd4, with clear compensation for the exchange) 19.♛g1, but after 19... ♜dc8 White still hasn't solved the issue of his c-pawn.

18...♝f8

The c5-pawn is falling, which leaves White with a strategically worse situation due to his split queenside.

Ivan embarks on kingside action, but he won't have the resources to carry out an attack.

19.f4 ♝xc5

Even better was 19...♜xd1+ 20.♜xd1 ♝xc5 21.♞d4 ♜d8, and White has no compensation for his ruined pawn structure.

20.♞d4 ♝f8 21.f5

21...♘xb3 I like this move. Although I reconnect White's pawns, it's more important to remove his strong bishop. The real weakness turns out to be White's e-pawn, which lacks a reliable defender.
22.axb3 e5

Fabiano Caruana's win against Ivan Cheparinov was a model game that any Grünfeld player should study.

Of course it's very important to drive White's knight from the centre and fix the e4-pawn. Exchanging on f5 would be a serious mistake.
23.♘f3 f6 24.c4 ♗c6 25.♕c2 ♖xd1+ After the trade of rooks White will have serious problems defending his pawns in the face of my light-squared bishop.
26.♖xd1 ♖d8 27.♖xd8 ♕xd8 28. fxg6 hxg6

29.♗xa7?
This seems like the decisive error. I suppose Ivan had overlooked or underestimated the strength of 30...b5. White just has to sit tight with 29. h3, when his position remains very unpleasant but with accurate play it might be defensible.
29...b6 30.c5 Forced. Otherwise the bishop will be lost.

30...b5! A very powerful move, which practically decides the game in Black's favour. White's bishop is trapped behind his own pawns, and contributes nothing to the fight, and after Black wins the e4-pawn the game will be over.
31.b4 Although White loses without a fight in the game, it's hard to find a single improvement for him. In a practical game White's task is nearly impossible.

31...♗h6

Patient play. I just improve my position and get ready to win e4.

32.♔g1 ♔g7 33.♔f2 ♕a8

34.♕a2 ♗xe4 35.♕a5 ♕b7 36. ♗b6 ♕d7 37.♕a7 ♗b7

Of course, endgames are also good for Black, but keeping the queens on will speed things up a bit. After ...e4 White will face a deadly attack.

38.♗d8 38.c6 ♗xc6 39.♕xd7+ ♗xd7 would only prolong the game a little bit. **38...e4 39.♘e1 ♕d2+**

40.♔g3 40.♔f1 ♗e3 41.♕xb7+ ♔h6 leads to mate.

40...♕f4+ After 41.♔h3 ♕f5+ 42. g4 ♕f1+ 43.♘g2 ♕f3+ it's all over, so White resigned.

NOTES BY
Ivan Sokolov

RL 10.5 – C79
David Navara
Ivan Sokolov
Reykjavik 2012 (5)

1.e4 e5 2.♘f3 ♘c6 3.♗b5 a6 4.♗a4

Over the last years (since writing *The Ruy Lopez Revisited* for New In Chess in 2009), I have extensively played Spanish 'sidelines', using the Jänisch, the Cozio (as in my Reykjavik game against Caruana), the Bird, the Smyslov or the Cordel variations, in order to take the game off the well-trodden paths as early as possible and to confront my opponents with an 'over-the-board' fight often as early as move 10 (or even, as in my game against Caruana, as early as move six!).

In the current booked up computer environment, this strategy (apart from occasional hiccoughs – which I would definitely have had with any variations!) has served me very well. Recently (anyhow, the last couple of tournaments), the delayed Steinitz and the Smyslov (3...g6) positions have mostly been in my focus. In this game I went for a hybrid move order (which had been rather popular in the 60s and then virtually disappeared from the top games) in order to achieve a good version of the Smyslov Variation for Black (side-stepping some unpleasant white options).

4...d6 5.0-0 ♘f6!? 6.♖e1

One of the two main white moves here, the other one being 6.c3.

6...♗d7 Over the board, I started to think that a transposition to a strange version of the Norwegian Variation may actually make sense for Black here: 6...b5!? 7.♗b3 ♘a5 8.d4.

ANALYSIS DIAGRAM

This particular position is normally not reached with a regular Norwegian Variation move order and (since I had not checked it before the game, as I only got this idea while playing) it was difficult for me to evaluate, so I decided to stick to my original 'war' plan.

However, the idea definitely deserves attention, e.g. 8...♘xb3 9.axb3 ♘d7, and it is far from an easy task to prove something tangible for White here: 10.dxe5 ♘xe5 11.♘xe5 (or 11.♗f4 ♘xf3+ 12.♕xf3 ♗e7 13.♘c3 ♗b7 14.♘d5 ♗xd5 15.exd5 0-0, and Black gradually equalizes) 11...dxe5 12.♕d5 (this greedy attempt may end in tears for White) 12...♕xd5 13.exd5 f6 14.f4 ♗d6 15.fxe5 fxe5 16.♘c3 ♗b7 17.♗f4 (White follows up on the 12.♕d5 idea and collects a pawn) 17...0-0 18.♗xe5 ♗c5+ 19.♔h1 ♖f2

ANALYSIS DIAGRAM

with certainly enough compensation for the pawn (and likely more):

20.♗xc7 ♗b4 21.♖ad1 ♖c8 22.♗e5 ♖xc2.

7.c3 g6 8.d4 b5 9.♗b3 ♗g7

I have now got the position I was aiming for – Black has a good version of the Smyslov Variation (White's most dangerous options have been side-stepped).

10.♗g5

Many, many strong grandmasters love to place this bishop on g5 in this type of position – a strategy I have never understood(!). It is utterly unclear to me what the white bishop is doing there – apart from executing a temporary (and quite harmless) pin, then later standing in White's way and ultimately being totally misplaced!

10...0-0

Since Black hasn't castled yet, I considered playing on the lousy bishop

immediately with 10...h6 11.♗h4 g5?! 12.♗g3 ♕e7 13.♘bd2 h5,

ANALYSIS DIAGRAM

but in the end I decided it would be way too risky due to 14.♘xg5! h4 15. ♗xf7+ (the computer suggests the strong 15.♗f4! exf4 16.♘xf7 ♖h5 – 16...♖f8 17.e5 winning – 17.♘f3, and Black may easily find himself on the receiving end of a brilliancy attack) 15...♔f8 16.♗xe5 dxe5 17.a4.

During the game this was enough to convince me to stay away from the idea to chase (and win) the white bishop. Chasing the bishop and hence weakening his kingside, Black actually often plays into White's hand, justifying the otherwise not dangerous bishop sortie to g5.

11.♘bd2 ♖e8

11...h6 12.♗h4 exd4 13.cxd4 g5 14.♗g3 ♘h5 was another idea, but

I wanted to leave the white bishop where it was.

12.h3?!

White is delaying central decisions and continues to keep the central tension (playing for 'an advantage').

12.dxe5 with approximate equality (after both 12...♘xe5 or 12...dxe5) is perhaps the sensible option for White here.

12.d5 ♘e7 leads to a double-edged position in which Black should definitely not be worse: Black is to develop a King's Indian type of kingside attack and most likely he has a rather favourable version compared to some Zaitsev lines, as the black dark-squared bishop is already on g7, while Black's light-squared bishop may well be better placed on d7 (than on b7).

12...h6 13.♗h4 ♘a5 14.♗c2 c5

With a fresh supply of coffee and coke, Ivan Sokolov is ready for a new adventure.

Black has an excellent Chigorin, and if someone should think about equality here, it is not Black.

15.♘b3 In case of 15.dxe5 dxe5 16. ♘f1, Black plays 16...♘c4. And 15.d5 ♕c7 looks like an OK Chigorin for Black.

15...cxd4 I did not want to play 15... ♘xb3 due to 16.♗xb3 (if 16.axb3 Black can continue as in the game: 16... cxd4 17.cxd4 exd4 18.♘xd4 ♕b6), and this position I was not sure about.

ANALYSIS DIAGRAM

However, closer examination shows that Black is actually doing quite well: 16...exd4 17.cxd4 g5! 18.♗g3 ♘xe4 19.♗d5 ♘xg3 (White would definitely rather have his pawn back on h2 here!) 20.♗xa8 ♖xe1+ 21.♕xe1 ♕xa8 22.fxg3 ♗xh3.

16.♘xa5
Or 16.cxd4 exd4! 17.♘bxd4 ♕b6 is again an excellent Chigorin for Black.
16...♕xa5 17.cxd4 exd4

18.♘xd4 This move he played quickly. It took me some time to establish that Black is doing excellently in case of 18.♕xd4 g5! (18...♘xe4?! 19.♕d5) 19.♕xd6 (19.♗g3 ♘xe4) 19...♗e6 20.♗g3 ♖ad8 21.♕a3 (the only move – 21.♕c7?? simply blunders a piece: 21...♕xc7 22.♗xc7 ♖c8) 21...♕xa3 22.bxa3 ♘h5, and Black will regain his material and have a better position.

18...♕b6
Black logically puts an accent on the pressure on the d4 square and the strong g7-bishop working on the h8-a1 diagonal. It is a good idea to take note of the terribly misplaced white 'active bishop' on h4, controlling a totally meaningless diagonal! Black has a dream Chigorin and White is worse here. The exploitation of Black's advantage has to be related to dynamic central pressure.

The other logical move for Black is 18...♖ac8, but I was not sure about the position after 19.♗b3, the most active white move, connected with a pawn sacrifice and the reason I did not go for ...♖c8. It transpires that Black can actually safely take the pawn!: 19... ♘xe4 20.♕f3

ANALYSIS DIAGRAM

20...♘g5! (a move I had missed in the game – the white ♖e1 is hanging and this makes all the difference!) 21. ♖xe8+ ♗xe8. Now the black f7-pawn is defended and White's compensation for the pawn should be insufficient.
19.♘f3
White removes his knight from the shaky square and creates the threat of e5.

19...♗e6

Eliminating that threat.

20.♘d4

20...♗c8!

The black bishop would be excellently placed on the a8-h1 diagonal.

21.♕d2 ♗b7 22.♗xf6 ♗xf6 23. ♖ad1

23...d5!

Black's central dynamic pressure is now maximal and Black's dynamic advantage quickly transforms into a more tangible one. Facing material loss, David tries to save the game with tactical tricks.

24.♗b3 ♖xe4 25.♖xe4 dxe4

26.♘f5!

By far the best practical chance for White here.

26...♖d8!

It would have been foolish to take the piece with 26...gxf5?, since after 27.♕xh6 White has (at least) a draw by perpetual check.

27.♘xh6+

Instead, 27.♘d6?? simply loses a piece after 27...♗g5 28.♗xf7+ (or 28.♕d4 ♕xd4 29.♖xd4 ♗e7) 28...♔f8 29.♕b4 ♗e7.

27...♔g7 28.♕c1 ♖xd1+ 29. ♗xd1

29...e3!

As expected, this move breaks White's coordination.

30.♘g4 exf2+ 31.♔f1

Black has a winning endgame in case of 31.♘xf2 ♕d4 32.♔f1 (32.b3? loses a piece after 32...♗h4) 32...♕xb2.

31...♗d4 32.♕h6+ ♔g8 33.♕f4

33...♕c6!

White is going to lose more material, so this concludes the game.

34.♗f3 ♕c4+ 35.♗e2 ♗xg2+ 36.♔xg2 ♕xe2 37.♘h6+ ♔h7

White resigned.

NOTES BY
Gawain Jones

KI 72.7 – E63
Stelios Halkias
Gawain Jones
Reykjavik 2012 (8)

After a very painful loss the previous evening to Boris Avrukh from a very pleasant position, I had to try and win Round 8 to finish anywhere in the prizes.

1.♘f3 ♘f6 2.d4 g6 3.g3

Deviating from our previous encounter at the European Team Championships. There he played the Gligoric Variation, but I quickly took over the initiative and managed to win. Unfortunately, that wasn't enough for the team, which went down 2½-1½.

3...♗g7 4.♗g2 0-0 5.c4 d6 6.0-0 ♘c6 7.♘c3 ♖b8

The main idea of this move order is to cut out the line suggested by Boris Avrukh: 8.♕d3.

7...a6 is the normal move order.

8.b3

8.♕d3 doesn't make sense anymore, as 8...e5 9.dxe5 dxe5 10.♕xd8 ♖xd8 11.♗g5 h6 12.♗xf6 ♗xf6 13.♘d5 ♗g7 14.♘xc7? no longer hits the rook, and after 14...e4 Black is much better.

8...a6 9.♗b2

With this logical developing move Halkias actually deviated from my previous games. Now I stopped to think for the first time and tried to remember any of my analysis.

In an earlier couple of games both

my opponents had tried 9.♘d5 e6 10.♘xf6+ ♕xf6 (10...♗xf6 11.♗h6 is a little awkward), but I'd managed to win both.

9...b5 10.cxb5

At this point we had our first off-the-board confrontation. Halkias wrote down his move and my recapture at the same moment, before I had actually replied myself. I calmly pointed out that I hadn't moved yet, and with a smile he scrubbed out my reply.

10...axb5 11.♖c1

This is an important strategic point in the game. Black has to come up with a good plan and find a use for the knight on c6. Still annoyed at myself from the previous day I failed to coordinate my pieces.

11...b4

Black generally plays a combination of this, ...♗d7 and a knight move off the c-file. It's unclear which of the two is the best move order.

The immediate 11...♘a5 worked well last year: 12.♘e1 ♗b7 13.e4 b4 14. ♘d5 ♘xe4! 15.♗xe4 e6 16.♗xg6?! hxg6 17.♘xb4 c5, and Black had a great position in Nyzhnyk-Vovk, Konya 2011.

12.♘a4 ♘a7

Within a few moves I was wishing I had placed my knight on a5, generally more normal in these structures. I hoped my knight had a better future on a7 – it can try to reroute itself via b5 – but the plan Halkias adopts of utilising the c4 square seems very strong.

12...♘a5 is probably better, although Black got into trouble in a recent GM game: 13.d5 e6?! (this doesn't work

Gawain Jones: 'At this point, I noticed something curious about how my opponent was notating.'

very well, so 13...♗d7 should probably be preferred) 14.dxe6 fxe6 15.♕c2 c5 16.♖fd1, with a position very similar to that of Aronian-Nakamura seen in the 13...e5 note. Black has a lot of problems defending his pawns. After 16... ♘b7 17.♘e5 ♕e8 18.♘c4 ♕e7, seen in Grachev-Bartel, Basel 2012, I'm sceptical as to whether Black has anything after 19.♗xb7 ♗xb7 20.♘xd6.

13.d5 And I think this is a good move. Otherwise Black will be able to play ...c6 and control some squares. Now, to create counterplay, Black will

have to break with either ...c5 or ...e5, both moves conceding something positionally. An exchange of c- and d-pawns would probably be ideal but it isn't so easy to achieve.

13...♗d7 I wasn't so sure about this move either, although it probably isn't so bad. I was playing on a kind of auto-pilot and soon my position descended into something horrible.

Black had no joy after 13...e5 in a high-powered blitz game: 14.dxe6 (playing as in the game with 14.♕d2, followed by 15.♘e1, also makes sense. I guess this is a slightly better version, as Black's bishop can go to b7 instead and put some pressure on d5, but White's still for preference) 14...fxe6 15.♕c2 c5?! (15...♘b5 was necessary, according to the silicon assistance) 16.♖fd1 ♕e7? 17.♖xd6!, and White had a decisive advantage in Aronian-Nakamura, Moscow 2010.

13...♗b7 was a move circulating somewhere in my head and was perhaps more interesting.

14.♘e1! After a long think Halkias came up with a strong plan of targeting my weak b4-pawn.
After 14.♘d4 e5 makes sense.

14...e5?!
I wasn't liking my position much already, but after this Black really struggles for counterplay.
Initially I had wanted to play 14...e6, but after 15.e4 I couldn't see a good follow-up. I contemplated 15...e5, but was a bit worried about White's subsequent f4 breaks, e.g. 16.♘d3 c5 17.f4 exf4 18.♖xf4, and White's better, but perhaps the computer's suggestion of 18...♗xa4 19.bxa4 ♘c8 is playable. At least I can hope for some queenside counterplay.

15.♘d3 15.♕d2 would have been a more accurate start, as it keeps d5 firmly protected and 15...♖b5 16.♖c4, followed by 17.♘c2, gives White a clear advantage.

15...♖b7? Blindness. After the long think on ...♖b5 I decided to play this 'safe' move.
I remember analysing 15...♖b5! but was uneasy about 16.♕c2 ♘xd5 17.♗xd5 ♖xd5 18.♕xc7, but apparently 18...♖a5! keeps Black's position together.

16.♖c4
Oops! After moving I realised I'd forgotten about this way of hitting the pawn, having only calculated 16.♕d2.

16...♕a8
A desperate attempt to get some kind of Benko Gambit compensation for the pawn, but in reality I'm simply a pawn down.
16...♕b8 17.♕d2 ♗xa4 18.bxa4 b3 would manage to keep material equality, but the bishop pair, the passed pawn and my terrible knight on a7 give White an overwhelming advantage.

17.♖xb4
The problem is that compared to a Benko Gambit my pawn structure is the wrong way round (e5 rather than c5), so my long-term positional compensation isn't really there.

17...♖fb8
I wanted to play 17...c5, but simply 18.dxc6 (18.♘b6!? is the computer's suggestion but at least this allows messiness, the one thing I crave!) 18...♗xc6 19.♗xc6 ♘xc6 20.♖xb7 ♕xb7 21.♕c2 keeps White fully in control.

18.♖xb7 ♕xb7 19.♗a1
At this point, I noticed something curious about how my opponent was notating. He would generally write something on his score sheet, think for another few minutes and then either move or cross it out and write something else, a clear no-no for the past few years. I remember when he played this move craning to see what he had written and only making out

'something 6' which confused and concerned me. As he was still thinking for a good 10 minutes after first writing down his 19th move, I went to the arbiter's desk and tried to explain the problem, and once he had moved I confronted him and reminded him that his action was illegal. He said he just wanted to play chess, and I replied, me too; I just want to play it by the rules. Had I been playing an old amateur player, I would have been tolerant, but a fairly young grandmaster should know the rules perfectly well. After this incident the rest of the game was played with a lot of nervous tension on both sides. At the end of the game he accused me of bringing this to light merely because I had a terrible position. While I can't contest my position was horrible, I felt uneasy with what seemed to be note-taking on his behalf and, after warning him already on move 10, would have complained regardless of the position.

19...♘b5 20.♕d2

20...h5!?
Unable to find a good plan and with both clocks running low already, I decided to start a grand old hack and at least give him practical problems.
20...♗f5, followed by putting something on e4, was my original intention, but I couldn't see a good plan after 21.♘b4, with the idea of sticking the knight in on c6.
21.♖c1 21.h4 would at least concede the g4 square, and actually after 21...♘d4 the computer doesn't completely hate my position.
21...h4
What else?

22.gxh4 Otherwise I can either exchange pawns on g3, followed by trying somehow to get a major piece to the h-file (perhaps with ...♕c8 and ...♗h3), or else play ...h3 and try to disturb his pieces a bit.
22...♕c8

23.♕e3?! With both of us down to around 10 minutes to last us until move 40, Halkias starts to panic.
23.♘b4! was strong, as 23...♗h3 24.♘c6 ♕g4 can be safely defused by 25.♕g5.
23...♗h7
I'm two pawns down and don't have any definite threats, but it's easy to get anxious on the white side.
24.♖c4?!
Overlooking my next.
24.f4 was my main line of analysis: 24...♗h6 25.♕f3! ♗f5, when 26.fxe5! is a very strong exchange sacrifice: 26...♗xc1 27.♘xc1 dxe5 28.♗xe5 ♘g4 29.♗f4 ♕a6 30.e4 ♕a7+ 31.♔f1, when the position is still messy but it feels good for White.
Meanwhile, 24.♕g5!? is the computer's curious suggestion. I have to admit that this move never crossed my mind!

24...♘a3 The rook is forced to retreat.

25.♖c1 So after White's error we have the same sort of ideas but with Black to move. However, it's not so easy to find a good way of playing.

25...♗f5
I think I spent around half my remaining time on this move. Again it's not clear what my last move achieved, but it keeps the tension and, with little time left, my opponent is forced to find a move.
Of course the first line to look at must be 25...♗h6 26.f4 ♘h5 (26...♗f5 would transpose to the game. I considered this move order but wanted to let him think over his next move), but following 27.♕f2 ♘xf4 28.♘xf4 exf4 I've only succeeded in winning one pawn back whilst opening the long diagonal for his bishop and losing my attack.
Of course 25...♘b5!? could be considered, but I didn't want to let him off his mistake.
26.f4 The most logical.
26.♕d2 is Rybka's suggestion, but I doubt it would be played by any carbon-based player, especially one low on time!
26...♗h6

27.♕a7?

Halkias forgets about my knight for the second time. This time the mistake is decisive.

During the game I worried about 27.♘xe5!? – White wrenches back the initiative, wins a couple of pawns and opens up the long diagonal for the a1-bishop: 27...dxe5 28.♕xe5 ♘g4 (28...♘d7 29.♕b2! ♘b5 30.e4 ♗g4 31.♕f2 leaves White with a great position) 29.♕e7 (taking the pawn immediately is a big error – 29.♕xc7? ♕e8!, with dual threats of ...♕e3+ and ...♖c8; 29.♕c3!? was a move I didn't consider, although it might be White's strongest) 29...♕e8 (during the game I dreamed I could play 29...♗xf4?!, but 30.♕xf7+ ♔h6 31.♕g7+ ♔h5 32.♕h7+ ♘h6 is surely too risky) 30.♖xc7,

ANALYSIS DIAGRAM

and here I could play on with 30...♗xf4! 31.♕xf7+ ♕xf7 32.♖xf7+ ♔g8 33.♖g7+ ♔f8, with a dynamically balanced position. White has four pawns for the piece but my f5, f4, g4 clump is quite strong.

27...♘b5

Defending c7 and attacking the queen. White has no option but to retreat.

28.♕f2 ♗xd3

29.fxe5?!

Objectively this move is just losing, but in huge time-trouble it wasn't so easy to convert.

29.exd3 ♘g4 30.♕f3 ♗xf4 31.♖c4 ♗xh2+ 32.♔h1 ♗f4 equalises material and would leave me with a much better structure and continuing attacking chances for free.

29...♗f5

The most straightforward. I remove one of my pieces from being attacked and block the f-file.

30.e4?!

Craziness! Halkias leaves the rook en prise and refuses to capture my piece too!

30.♖c4 was the best try, preventing me from playing ...♘g4, although now 30...dxe5 31.♗xe5 ♕e8! is winning, as 32.♗xf6 ♗e3 picks up the queen.

30...♘g4 31.♕g3 ♗xc1

32.e6

Taking the bishop leaves me in a trivially winning position a rook up, so he tries to confuse me.

32...♗xe6 33.h5 ♗e3+ 34.♔h1 ♘f2+

The start of a series of checks designed to get to the time-control.

35.♔g1 ♘g4+ 36.♔h1 ♘f2+ 37.♔g1 ♘d1+ 38.♔h1 ♘d4 39.♘c3 ♘f2+ 40.♔g1 ♘g4+

Time-control reached and an extra 30 minutes to make sure I don't allow any cheapos.

41.♔h1 ♘f2+ 42.♔g1 ♘h3+ 43.♔h1 ♗f2 44.hxg6+ fxg6 45.♕d3 ♗g4 46.e5 ♕f5

Halkias decided he'd had enough and, summoning the arbiter, informed him he wished to resign but not to shake my hand and complained that I had distracted him on purpose by forcing him to stick to the rules.

A game with many mistakes, but at least it was entertaining!

NOTES BY
Hou Yifan

SI 47.3 – B22
Vladimir Baklan
Hou Yifan
Reykjavik 2012 (8)

This was my first time in Iceland, to take part in one of the world's great traditional open tournaments – the Reykjavik Open. I really liked the playing venue. The view from the playing table was the ocean, which always put me in a good mood ☺! This was also my first game against GM Baklan.
1.e4 c5 2.c3 ♘f6 3.e5 ♘d5 4.♘f3 ♘c6 5.♗c4 e6 6.0-0 d6 7.d4 cxd4 8.cxd4 ♗e7 9.♕e2 0-0 10.♖d1 ♘a5 11.b3!?
This move serves two purposes: to keep the bishop on c4 for the moment and then to decide to withdraw it or to take on d5, depending on Black's next move; and to allow the c1-bishop to go to a3, which is a better square than f4 to attack the d6 pawn.

11...♗d7 I understood that this move would waste a tempo later on, but I thought it was not a big deal. Most of the choices here will lead to similar positions as after the game continuation: 11...a6!? 12.♗xd5 exd5 13.♘c3 ♗e6, or 11...b6 12.♗xd5 exd5 13.♘c3 ♗e6 14.♗a3.
Not so good is 11...♘xc4?! 12.bxc4 ♘b4 13.exd6 ♗xd6 14.♘c3, when Black has the bishop pair, but the disadvantage of the position is obvious: the light-squared bishop still needs some time to join the play, the knight

on b4 is a little strangely placed, and in the meantime White has developed almost all his pieces to control the centre with his central pawns.
12.♗xd5 exd5 13.♘c3 ♗e6 14. ♗a3 a6 15.h3 ♖e8 16.♕d3 ♘c6 17.♖e1 h6 18.♖ac1 ♖c8 19.exd6 ♗xd6 20.♗xd6 ♕xd6 21.♘e5

21...♘e7!?
After a series of normal moves the position is more or less equal. The only problem that caught my eye is that if I agree to exchange the knight this will lead to an active knight vs. bad bishop ending, with a dangerous position for me, for example: 21...♕a3 22.♘xc6 ♖xc6 23.♖cd1 ♕d6 24.♘a4 a5. But maybe I'm being over-cautious.
In this position I found two active plans for Black: ...f6, ...♗f5, ...♘g6 and ...♘f4 to exert pressure on the kingside, or ...♘f5 to attack the d4-pawn and, above all, prevent ♘d3-c5. Frankly speaking, I preferred the first possibility.
22.♕d2 ♘f5
Obviously, the first plan that I mentioned is not suitable here: 22...f6 23.♘d3, and the knight occupies an excellent square from where it can control the c5 and f4 squares.
23.♘e2 ♖xc1 24.♖xc1 f6

25.♘f3
Maybe my opponent was a little worried about the d4 pawn if he continued his original idea (♘d3), but this return doesn't look right, as he wastes two tempi.
Better was 25.♘d3!? ♗f7 26.♘c5 b6 27.♘a4 ♕e7 28.♘g3! ♕xg3 29.fxg3 ♕d6 30.♕f4 ♕b4, when Black is only slightly better.
25...♗f7 26.♖e1

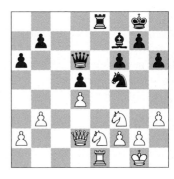

26...h5!? An interesting idea aimed at activating my last piece on the board with the subsequent ...h4, ...♗h5.
27.♘c3 ♖c8

28.♘a4!?
Preventing the sortie ...♕b4. Another choice here was 28.♖c1 g5 29.♘e2 ♖xc1+ 30.♕xc1 ♔g7, and although Black has the initiative on the kingside, White has no clear weakness, and it would not be easy to improve my position.
28...b5
Interesting was 28...♕c7!?, taking control of the c-file first and waiting for a good opportunity to push ...b5: 29.♖d1 b5 30.♘b2 ♕c3 31.♘d3 ♕xd2 32.♖xd2 g5 33.g4 ♘d6 34.♘c5, and the black knight comes to e4.

Reykjavik 2012

					TPR
1	Fabiano Caruana	ITA	2767	7½	2777
2	Ivan Sokolov	NED	2653	7	2744
3	David Navara	CZE	2700	7	2709
4	Gawain Jones	ENG	2635	7	2697
5	Boris Avrukh	ISR	2591	7	2667
6	Hou Yifan	CHN	2639	7	2677
7	Sebastien Mazé	FRA	2577	7	2569
8	Henrik Danielsen	ISL	2504	7	2574
9	Ivan Cheparinov	BUL	2664	6½	2695
10	Robert Hess	USA	2635	6½	2638
11	Erwin l'Ami	NED	2611	6½	2543
12	Yury Kryvoruchko	UKR	2666	6½	2594
13	Hannes Stefansson	ISL	2531	6½	2541
14	Vasily Papin	RUS	2575	6½	2489
15	Vladimir Baklan	UKR	2612	6½	2578
16	Aloyzas Kveinys	LTU	2512	6½	2474
17	Hedinn Steingrimsson	ISL	2556	6½	2497
18	Stelios Halkias	GRE	2588	6½	2494
19	Kore Akshayraj	IND	2422	6	2563
20	Yury Kuzubov	UKR	2615	6	2543
21	Hjorvar Gretarsson	ISL	2460	6	2513
22	Andreas Moen	NOR	2360	6	2431
23	Alexander Ipatov	TUR	2561	6	2484
24	Alina l'Ami	ROU	2372	6	2414
25	Simon Williams	ENG	2506	6	2462
26	Jens Kristiansen	DEN	2432	6	2403
27	Irina Krush	USA	2461	6	2457
28	Fabien Libiszewski	FRA	2523	6	2406
29	Helgi Dam Ziska	FAI	2456	6	2431
30	Sigurdur Sigfusson	ISL	2346	6	2378
31	Marc Arnold	USA	2502	6	2414
32	Keaton Kiewra	USA	2355	6	2353
33	Yuri Shulman	USA	2594	6	2317
34	Ian Thompson	ENG	2255	6	2273

150 players, 9 rounds

29.♕d3 A little surprise! I only calculated 29.♘b2 h4 30.♖c1! ♖e8 31. ♖e1 ♖xe1+ 32.♘xe1 and the weaker 29.♘c5?! ♘xd4 30.♘xd4 ♕xc5, which doesn't seem to give enough compensation for the pawn and which may be even worse than the game.

29...♕f4! 30.♘c5?!
The solid 30.♘c3 ♘d6 31.g3 ♕f5 would have been a better choice here. **30...♘xd4 31.♘xd4 ♖xc5 32.g3 ♕c7 33.♕d2**

Taking stock in this position, we see that Black has an extra pawn on d5, while the light-squared bishop may at some stage occupy the weak h1-e4 diagonal. On the other hand, d4 is a powerful square for the white knight, which is White's only hope.

33...♕c8?!
Preparing the manoeuvre ...♗g6-e4, while at the same time controlling the c-file. But the move is a bit too hasty, as it gives up the defence of the seventh rank. My first step should have been 33... ♖c3! 34.♔g2 b4 35.♖e2 ♕d6 (after 35...♗g6 White has 36.♘f5!, a combination Black has to pay attention to, as I would find out in the game).
My first thought during the game was 33...h4, but it's not the best choice: 34. gxh4 ♖c3 35.♔g2 ♗h5 36.♖e3.
34.♔h2 ♗g6 35.♖e7 ♖c7?!

36.♘f5! A nice combination which I had missed! It made me anxious under time-pressure and, above all, caused my next huge blunder.

36...♕d8?
The only move to keep winning chances was 36...♖d7! 37.♖xd7 (37.♕e3!? ♗f7) 37...♕xd7 38.♕xd5+ ♕xd5 39.♘e7+ ♔f7 40.♘xd5 ♗e4! 41.♘c3 ♗f3!.

ANALYSIS DIAGRAM

A weird position, Black is almost winning here, for instance: 42.♔g1 ♔e6 43.♔f1 ♔e5 44.♘e2 ♗xe2+ 45.♔xe2 ♔d4 46.♔d2 b4.

37.♖xc7
The right move was 37.♕a5!. After the game my opponent told me he saw this move at that point but had forgotten that his king had already moved to h2, so there's no check on c1! Now 37...♕xe7 is the only move: 38.♘xe7+ ♖xe7 39.♕xa6 d4 40.♕d6 ♖e1 41.♕b4! ♖e2 42.♕xd4 ♖xa2 43.♕d5+ ♔h8 44.♔g1, and it will be very difficult to save this position. There's no hope of exchanging the b-pawns, which is the only drawing opportunity here.

37...♕xc7 38.♕xd5+ ♔h7 39. ♘e3
An easier way to equality was 39.♔g2 ♕c2 40.g4! hxg4 41.hxg4 ♕xa2 42.♕d7.

39...♕a5 40.a4 ♕e1 41.♕f3

This endgame is easy to play for Black because of White's weaknesses on the kingside and the light-squared pawns, but actually this is an almost equal position.
41...b4 42.g4 h4!

43.♘f5?
A last mistake and the losing move. He should have played 43.♔g2 ♕b1 44.♘f5 ♗f7 45.♘d4 a5, although the position remains better for Black.
43...♗f7!
I found it hard to decide between the text-move and 43...♕c3. In the end, I decided to exchange the h4 pawn against b3, which would give me a passed pawn, an essential element of the win. After 43...♕c3, play could continue 44.♕d1 (44.♔g2 ♗f7) 44...♗f7 45.♘d4 g6 to provide a safe place for the king and then to try and bring the bishop into play.
44.♘xh4 ♕e5+ 45.♔g1 ♕d5

Hou Yifan: 'The view of the ocean always put me in a good mood ☺!'

After a few only moves the position

is clear: the b3 pawn is about to fall.
46.♕e2 The attempt to muddy the waters with 46.♕f4 cannot change the outcome: 46...g5 47.♕xf6 gxh4 48.♕xh4+ ♔g6, and White is at the end of his tether.
46...♕xb3 47.♕e4+ g6 48.♕e7 ♔g7 49.g5 fxg5 50.♕e5+ ♔h7 51.♕xg5 ♕d1+ 52.♔h2 ♕d6+ 53.♔g1 b3 54.♕c1 ♕f6 55.♕c7 b2 56.♕b7 ♔h6 57.♘f3 ♗a2
White resigned. ∎

'I leave this to you'

EINAR EINARSSON

Helgi Olafsson listens to Bobby Fischer on the first night that they met, on April 2, 2005.

'I leave this to you.' These were the last words that Bobby Fischer whispered before he slipped into unconsciousness and died in Reykjavik's Landsspitalinn on January 17, 2008. Having resisted any kind of operation to treat the degenerative renal failure he was suffering from and refusing to take any medicine, the American world champion also chose to fight his last battle alone. Now he resigned. Never before had the doctors seen a patient put up such a stubborn and determined fight. The only relief from the terrible pain he must have been in, came from the opium plasters that the nurses used without him knowing it.

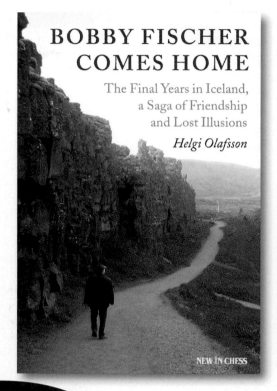

B Bobby Fischer's last words are revealed in *Bobby Fischer Comes Home*, a book on his final years in Iceland, written by Icelandic grandmaster Helgi Olafsson.

The words most often cited in connection with Fischer's final days are those he spoke to psychiatrist Magnus Skulason, when the latter sat at his bedside two days before his death and tried to ease his pain by massaging his feet. According to Skulason Fischer said 'with a terrible gentleness' 'Nothing is as healing as the human touch', beautiful words that indeed deserve to be quoted.

In Olafsson's book we read that Skulason was emotionally devastated after Fischer's death. 'He made a reference to the crucifixion of Christ and spoke bitterly about those who had betrayed Bobby.' Another member of the group around Fischer in Iceland also drew a parallel with Christ's crucifixion when he learned from a reliable source what his last words had been. He was reminded of the last words Christ is supposed to have said: 'Father, into your hands I commit my spirit.'

Such lofty thoughts were not on Helgi Olafsson's mind and they would not have been in line with the feet-on-the-ground friendship he had with Fischer. A friendship that he could not have dreamed of when as a 15-year-old boy he breathlessly followed the Match of the Century in Reykjavik in 1972. At that time Olafsson was living on the Westman Islands south of Iceland, but he nevertheless managed to see a number of the games in Laugardalshöll and even got access to the press room.

When in July 2004 Bobby Fischer was arrested in Japan, Olafsson was one of the members of the RJF Committee that set out to free the American and prevent his extradition to the U.S. where without the shadow of a doubt he would be sentenced to a long term in prison as punishment for the controversial match he played against Spassky in war-torn Yugoslavia in 1992.

Once the Icelandic parliament granted Fischer Icelandic citizenship, the road to freedom was opened and on March 24, 2005, after nine months in a Japanese detention centre, Bobby Fischer returned to the country where 33 years earlier he had celebrated his greatest triumph.

During Fischer's detention in Japan, Olafsson had sent him three chess books (Pablo Moran's *Agony of a Genius*, Edward Winter's *Capablanca* and Andy Soltis' *Soviet Chess*) and perhaps it was because of this token of sympathy and support that the American wanted to meet him when he arrived in Iceland. At their first meeting the conversation was mostly small talk, but then at a Welcome Bobby dinner they enthusiastically exchanged stories. At the end of the evening Fischer asked Olafsson for his mobile telephone number. As Olafsson writes matter-of-

factly: 'From then on he would start calling me on a regular basis.' Soon Fischer would be calling him almost every day and a unique friendship developed. They would go out for dinner, go to the movies, make trips around Reykjavik and outside the city, play pool, have fun and have disagreements. And, yes, they also played chess, Fischer-Random that is, naturally.

Bobby Fischer Comes Home is the story of their friendship. With a keen eye for detail and a fine sense of humour, Olafsson paints a portrait of a complicated person. A man who could be at times funny and good-humoured, at times bitter and barely bearable, almost always suspicious, but also touching, spontaneous and fun to be with. Filled with unforgettable scenes and revealing insights, the book presents a compelling picture of the last years of the man who many see as the greatest chess player that ever lived.

To whet your appetite we publish a chapter of the book, in which Bobby Fischer goes on a fishing trip with three Icelanders, one of them being, needless to say, the author. ●

Helgi Olafsson

He said, 'Wither away, Skarphedinn?'
'We shall fish for salmon, father.'
Njal's Saga

A

All sorts of people wanted to meet Bobby Fischer in the first days and weeks after his arrival in Iceland, and Bobby would talk freely to almost anyone. Viggo Hilmarsson was a senior manager at Straumur, an Icelandic investment bank. Bobby would later call him a 'bankster', but that was all right with Viggo. He was the only son of Hilmar Viggoson, who had been a member of the Icelandic Chess Federation during the 1972 match.

Viggo's father may well have told his son a few bedtime stories about the Great Match. I met him outside my home in early May 2005. We had met on another occasion at least once and I knew he was a keen follower of chess and a strong amateur player. Viggo asked for my assistance. A Canadian friend of his very much wanted Bobby to autograph a copy of *My 60 Memorable Games*. When I spoke with Bobby he was readily willing to sign the book. But he refused to sign the Faber & Faber copy I had brought him.

'It has to be a Simon and Schuster', he said. I didn't feel like asking him for the reason, but I knew the original publisher had been Simon & Schuster. The publication rights had been sold to Faber & Faber and the latest twist was when Batsford bought the rights from Faber & Faber and published an edition with the games in algebraic notation in 1995. According to the chess historian Edward Winter, British grandmaster John Nunn, who prepared the text for Batsford, made some 560 textual changes to the book. Fischer was furious about the Batsford edition and called the Batsford team 'criminals' and 'conspirators' at a press conference in Buenos Aires in 1996.

Probably the most painful change in the Batsford edition was a 'corrected' variation in Bobby's game against Bolbochan from the Stockholm interzonal of 1962. In the 'improved' line a check was overlooked that made the entire variation nonsensical.

In any case I brought a copy of the Simon & Schuster hardback to Bobby's suite at the Hotel Loftleidir. Before he signed the book he asked: 'Is he a good person, this man?' 'Oh yes, I think so', I answered. Inside the book there was a one thousand krona bill, worth about 12 euros. Bobby smiled and put it in his wallet. Then he slowly signed the book.

Viggo was living with his wife above café Mokka in 101 Reykjavik. I knew the flat did not suit Bobby, but Viggo contacted me and said that he was willing to rent it to Bobby for a modest price as he and his wife had plans to build a house on the outskirts of Reykjavik. I went there with Bobby to take a look and he and Viggo got along fine. Viggo and his wife later invited Bobby to dinner and Viggo suggested that one day they could go fishing. In the end Bobby did not rent Viggo's apartment.

One day Viggo called me and proposed a fishing trip with Bobby. I knew he had gone fishing in a salmon river called Laxa in Kjos after the match in 1972. Bobby accepted the invitation and agreed to come with us. The trip took place at the end of August 2005.

Viggo Hilmarsson shows his skills at fly fishing.

The salmon river GIjufura runs through the northwestern part of Iceland. The best part of summer in Iceland for salmon fishing is usually July, but in this area you can expect to be quite successful in August or even the early part of September.

Viggo had initially intended to invite just me and Bobby, but I insisted that a friend of mine, an actor by the name of Johann Sigurdarson, should also come along. This turned out to be a good idea. We decided that Johann and I would pick Bobby up from his flat in Klapparstigur. Bobby let us in and Miyoko was there. She had arrived from Japan the night before. Apparently Bobby had not told her about the fishing trip.

Miyoko was living in Japan, but would come to Iceland every two or three months and stay there for at least ten days. She had met Bobby the year after he became World Champion during his Asia trip in the fall of 1973. At the time she was studying pharmacy and later she graduated as a master of science. Afterwards she became the president of the Japanese Chess Federation and was working there full time as a general secretary when Bobby got in touch with her whilst living in Budapest.

'But I came yesterday', Miyoko said smilingly. 'This was planned months

ahead', Bobby insisted, slightly apologetically. It was probably the only time I sensed some guilt on Bobby's part. I wondered whether we should also invite Miyoko, but the small size of the self-catering lodge that came with the fishing permit could have been a real obstacle. Besides, Viggo wasn't there, so I did not mention this possibility. Bobby kept on mumbling something, no hug or kisses, but then finally he waved Miyoko goodbye.

We made a stop at a shopping mall. As I went into a store for supplies, Bobby sat in the café on the first floor with Johann. Soon Bobby would start calling him Big Joe. When I came back half an hour later they were deep in conversation. Joe told me that while I had been shopping Bobby had received a phone call from his Icelandic lawyer, and now there was a serious change of mood. As we drove away I heard for the first time about Bobby's correspondence with the Swiss bank UBS, where he kept his earnings from the 1992 match. Bobby told us that shortly after his arrival in Iceland he had received a letter from UBS in which all business relations between the parties involved were terminated. As a result all his assets would be liquidated and sent to Landsbankinn, the national bank of Iceland. Bobby's lawyer had allowed UBS to make this transfer and this had enraged Bobby. We had to do some more shopping and I rather casually suggested that this turn of events had also been caused by pressure from abroad, most probably from the U.S. Justice Department.

'Of course. Goes without saying!' Bobby shouted back. He was becoming very irritated. Joe tried to explain to him that we were just trying to gather information. I 'blundered' horribly about his Icelandic lawyer when I asked: 'Is he on a commission or something?' This enraged Bobby even further, but I tried to keep calm since I knew that sometimes lawyers get a percentage of the amount at stake. We drove on and for the next 200 kilometres or so Bobby would not talk about anything but the UBS bank and we took a few 'punches' on behalf of the gigantic Swiss bank. At one point he called Landsbankinn and talked with a senior official from the bank. She confirmed that the bank had received a notice from UBS and a few million Swiss francs had been transferred to an account in his name in Landsbankinn. Bobby was furious: 'Send it back', he told the woman.

Our first stop was at a roadhouse café near a village built around the university at Bifrost. There we had a cup of coffee, Bobby ordered tea and kept on talking about the UBS bank. Our next stop was at a roadhouse café close to a bridge over Hrutarfjardar river, one of the more expensive salmon rivers in Iceland. Outside we spotted a leather-clad biker who looked familiar. 'Didn't we once play badminton with this guy?' I asked Joe. His name was Otto Jonsson and he was riding a Harley Davidson Road King from Reykjavik, heading north.

When he noticed that Joe was waving at him he walked to the car, had a few words with me and Joe but soon turned his attention to our sullen passenger in the front seat. It transpired that Otto had studied medicine in New York. 'So you were in the jungle', Bobby said, warming by the minute to the new acquaintance. 'Right. I was in the jungle.'

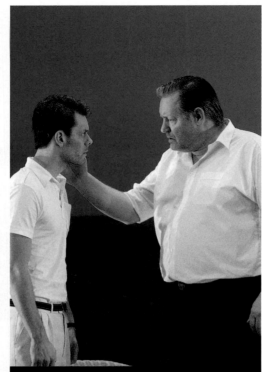

Johann 'Big Joe' Sigurdarson in Arthur Miller's *All My Sons* at the Icelandic National Theatre.

Bobby laughed, and they had a pleasant conversation. Bobby could start a conversation with almost anyone. For us the important thing was that from then on the UBS matter was dropped. Not a word about it for the rest of the fishing trip.

We arrived late at the fishing hut and early the next morning we went fishing. We put a fishing rod into Bobby's hands. He was already in his boots and was armed with a tackle box, sunglasses, cap, gloves and sunscreen. The salmon rivers in Iceland are broken into sections, or beats, and each section has a story of its own, as is documented in the many river guides. Viggo went with Bobby to a spot very close to the fishing hut. Joe drove alone in his jeep. I stayed away, close to the fishing hut, practicing my golf swing. I had lost all interest in fishing long ago.

In less than five minutes Bobby's fishing rod all of a sudden began swinging and pumping furiously. Bobby's hands were trembling. 'Viggo, what the hell shall I do?' he shouted. 'Raise the fishing

rod immediately!' Viggo shouted back.

Bobby had stumbled upon a remarkably stubborn salmon, but with Viggo's help they managed to land it in 15 minutes. When I walked over from the hut to where they were fishing it was Viggo's turn to try, but Bobby was pacing on the banks of the river watching Viggo's every move.

'So, what have you been up to?' I asked. 'I caught this one', Bobby answered, and pointed at the six-pounder. He was very quiet and looked like an ordinary fisherman on the banks of a river who had teamed up with an old friend.

At noon there was the customary break. We went into the fishing hut, where Bobby's catch was celebrated with a shot of whisky. After the break I asked Bobby if he was going to try again. 'No,' he said, 'I am very happy with just one salmon. It's enough for me.' Big Joe and Viggo tried harder and were quite successful. When they came in at eight o'clock in the evening I prepared dinner for us, which was my own version of Spaghetti Bolognese with parmesan cheese, bread and a salad and some red wine. This was followed by a dessert.

At one point during dinner Bobby looked at me and said: 'This is good', something I had to take as a compliment. Big Joe had brought his guitar with him and a book of notes and lyrics. Soon after dinner he and Bobby started to jam. Bobby knew all the lyrics. We wondered how he had learned them so well. 'I was just listening to the radio', he said. 'But you must have had some records', I insisted. 'I think I once bought a record', Bobby said.

Big Joe has a well-trained voice. He has had leading roles in the National Theatre in musicals like *Les Misérables*, *Fiddler on the Roof* and *The Sound of Music*. He has also sang in the opera a few times, and has been a member of a few bands. So Bobby was jamming with a pro. Still, he almost shouted when he thought Joe was singing out of tune.

'No, no, no. This is corny', he said, and proceeded to demonstrate how the song should be sung. He was very impressed by Big Joe. 'Do you know who my favourite radio host was? Big Joe Junior. He would come on late at night and this was his favourite sentence: "For anyone. You may be alone out there, but we are happy together."'

I envisioned the young Bobby Fischer alone in his Brooklyn flat listening to this disk jockey. Joe Rosenfield was the host of a radio talk show called 'The Happiness Exchange' for many years. He was also known as Big Joe, and his night-time show was called 'The Insomnia Stretch'. It was broadcast on several New York radio stations.

On many occasions 'our' Big Joe has been asked for a few Frank Sinatra standards. This evening he started out with *New York, New York* and then it was *My Way*. 'Regrets, I had a few...' 'Hey, this song is about Bobby', Viggo said. We got the point. Bobby was quiet for a while. He was bowing his head.

'C'mon Bobby. Don't be shy', I teased him a bit. When we made way for the old Tom Jones standard *Green, Green Grass of Home*, it turned out we had totally misunderstood the lyrics. 'You see, the guy is waiting for his execution in a cell and the old padre is paying him the final visit before he is to be taken before the firing squad', Bobby explained to us.

At this point I opened the door and I noticed that it was a clear sky with millions of stars visible, and the northern lights were in full bloom. I called Bobby: 'Bobby. Have you ever seen the northern lights?' I asked him. He went out and gazed at the stars and this phenomenon that sometimes looks like curtains glowing above. He stood there for a very long time.

Shortly afterwards we took a walk outside the fishing hut. It was not much of an effort, but he was breathing heavily and I wondered about the status of his health. Then we returned. Bobby and Big Joe sang a few more standards and then Joe went to bed. But Bobby kept singing alone for a while. It was pitch dark, we had extinguished all the lights, but he kept pacing the floor of the fish-

PALL G. JONSSON

After the 1972 match Bobby Fischer went fishing for salmon in the Laxa river together with Miguel Quinteros.

ing hut singing to himself. He was not a bad singer, but as I was lying in my bed I thought, when is this guy going to stop singing?

When I opened my eyes in the morning Bobby was already up. He was walking around the fishing hut talking to himself: 'The fucking Jews, they are after me, I must get to them. The fucking Jews.' And on and on. It was disturbing. Did he wake up every morning, day after day, week after week, year after year talking to himself like this?

I knew Bobby liked conspiracy theories, so I had brought a book with me about the JFK assassination, *Case Closed* by Gerald Posner, which I 'accidentally' left

on my bed. He now turned his attention to the book and started to read. I told Bobby that I agreed with Posner's theories that Lee Harvey Oswald had acted alone.

'By the way, Bobby. Where were you when you heard about the assassination?' I asked. 'I was in my apartment in Brooklyn', Bobby replied. 'Let me see. Gerald Posner. The name suggests that he is from Poland. So I think there is a good chance he is a Jew.' After a while Bobby got tired of the book, but stated that it was highly unlikely that the theories put forward in it could hold water.

At about 12 o'clock we started to prepare for our departure. The rule was to leave the fishing hut in exactly the same condition as when we had arrived. Some work had to be done, washing the dishes and mopping the floor. Bobby participated in full. Everything was in order when we left the hut. Joe asked Bobby to sign for the fish he had caught in a special notebook. 'This is the custom in the salmon rivers of Iceland', he said. 'Nah, I don't think so', Bobby answered. 'Come on, Bobby you have to do it. Do it for us', I said. And Bobby Fischer signed for the salmon, a six-pounder. In the fishing record book he wrote: 'R. Fischer. Catch: salmon. Weight: 6 pounds.' Little could he know at that point that the proprietors of the river decided several years after his death to name the spot where he caught the fish after him.

When we came back to Reykjavik, Miyoko was waiting for us. Bobby had phoned her on his mobile several times during the trip. We brought with us a big box with Bobby's catch. He opened it and proudly offered the fish to Miyoko. Like any other Japanese woman Miyoko knew how to handle a fish. She wet her hands and then stored it in the refrigerator. Afterwards she washed her hands with lukewarm soapy water.

'We must go fishing again soon', Big Joe said to Bobby. 'Yes, of course. Let's go again next week', he replied excitedly. I was very relieved. He had enjoyed the trip. ■

Beware, TN!!

Chess Informant's publication _1000 TN!!_ provides a guided tour of more than 40 years of creativity in the openings. Hans Ree was guided through memory lane.

I t must have been in 1978 that an acquaintance who saw me on a pavement terrace, burst out into spontaneous laughter when he got a glimpse of what I was reading before saying a word to me. It was volume E of the Yugoslav _Encyclopedia of Chess Openings_, which I had just bought. He may have thought that I was trying to memorize everything on the densely printed pages and may have found that as quaint as learning the Amsterdam telephone directory by heart.

I didn't mind his hilarity. He was an editor of the weekly magazine where I had a chess column, and if he thought of me as a weird nerd, he would at least realize that I took my trade seriously.

Of course I didn't memorize or even read all the lines, but as a conscientious student of the _Chess Informant_s I knew more or less what I would find in their encyclopedia and where I would have to look to find material that might be

relevant to weak spots in my opening repertoire.

'I read it just for entertainment, as you might read a Donald Duck story,' I said to my editor. That was not quite true, but indeed, reading chess literature was more a pleasure than an effort. I was on familiar ground, confident that if I missed something, it wouldn't be very important.

One big hole

Recently I have been browsing through another product of Sahovski Informator, the Serbian company that has published the _Informant_s since 1966. Starting with volume 11, the _Informant_ has printed a list of the ten best novelties of the previous volume, selected by a panel of top players. A hundred of these lists, together with the corresponding games, have now been collected in the book _1000 TN!! – The Best Theoretical Novelties_, a hefty tome of 638 pages. It goes from _Informant_ 11 to 110 and covers the period between the end of 1970 and 2010.

Of course I had seen many of these novelties, not only when I was a professional player, but also in more recent years. But I can no longer connect them to a solid body of knowledge. My opening repertoire doesn't have holes; it is one big hole in which a few tiny threads of half-forgotten knowledge are floating around. I go as a tourist through an area where I once lived and where everything has changed.

One, but a lion

'Nothing excites jaded grandmasters more than a theoretical novelty,' wrote Dominic Lawson in his book _The Inner Game_ (1993) about the world championship match between Garry Kaspa-

rov and Nigel Short. Lawson obviously disliked chess grandmasters, jaded or not, and one of his favourite objects of disdain was the late and much-missed Tony Miles. Therefore Lawson might find it fitting that on the back cover of _1000 TN!!_ a position is shown in which Miles produced a startling and devastating novelty against Alexander Beliavsky in Tilburg in 1986.

18.f4, and according to John Nunn's analysis, Black is already a goner. This move was missed by White in the sixth match game of Kasparov-Timman in Hilversum in 1985, though it strikes me as a typical Kasparov move.

It was the one occasion in 40 years when all nine members of the panel were unanimous in their choice of the best novelty of the previous _Informant_. It was the only time that Miles won top honours, but as the lion said when the mouse asked him how many children he had: 'One, but a lion.'

Actually, there is no truth to Lawson's snide remark, as it is certainly not the jaded grandmasters who are excited by a novelty, but the sprightly and ambitious grandmasters who are keen on sharpening their weapons. The jaded grandmaster will only be in fear of novelties, assuming he would recognize one if he came across it.

Bobby wanted it clean

When the first *Informant* appeared in 1966, it was immediately obvious to almost all serious players that the series would be an essential tool in their opening preparation and that we couldn't afford to miss one issue. Every volume provided a few hundred important recent games that we would otherwise have had to collect from *Shakhmatny Bulletin* or other magazines. This sentence slipped from my pen, but actually I now realize that at that time, when I was 21 years old, I received very few chess magazines. They were just too expensive.

At the time, I was pleased to find that the first volume showed two nice games by me, victories over Bent Larsen and Helmut Pfleger. Pity that the editors didn't make it clear that they were played in a little tournament that I had won, in the small Dutch town of Ter Apel. It was only indicated that the games had been played in The Netherlands, and for all the readers knew, my win against Larsen might as well have taken place in a simul that he had given.

Indications of places and circumstances were very sketchy in general in that first volume, and most annotations consisted only of a few question marks or exclamation marks and an occasional suggestion of an alternative move. The series has gone a long way since.

Very soon the volumes, appearing twice a year at that time, expanded. All kinds of sections were added, for instance endgame positions and positions in which a nice combination was executed. And indeed, why not?

But Bobby Fischer didn't like it. When I met him at the tournament in Netanya, Israel, in 1969, he expressed his disappointment. 'They had it set up so nice and clean and now they're spoiling it.' He was a purist who wanted to have just the game notations, no thrills and frills to beautify the basic materials for the masses.

A late convert

I mentioned that almost all serious players realized the importance of the *In-formant* right from the start, but there is at least one exception. During the Olympiad in Nice in 1974 the Dutch grandmaster Hein Donner excitedly told his fellow team members that he had found something fantastic in a bookstall outside the playing hall. A publication that had hundreds of important games from the preceding six months. We should take a look.

We were stunned. Did he mean the *Informant*? Obviously he did. Was he joking or had he really not been aware of its existence before? He wasn't joking. Between 1966 and 1974 Donner had played in the most prestigious tournaments, beating World Champions Spassky and Smyslov, and all that time he had been unaware of the most important tool of the trade.

When preparing for an Olympiad, the Dutch team members had already had the habit of discussing in advance who would put which *Informant* in his suitcase for general use. A few opening books, Chéron's endgame volumes and the most recent *Informants*; that was the minimum luggage that the team would take, while everybody would add some literature to his individual liking. But Donner had never been present at these discussions.

What heights would Donner have reached if he had been aware of the *Informants* and had studied them? But he would still have been handicapped by the fact that he didn't have a chess board and pieces at home.

Zdenko Krnic

Through the years I became bound to the *Informant*, not only as a customer, but also as a contributor. At important tournaments we knew we would meet Zdenko Krnic, who would come to ask us for annotated games and pay for the

annotations that we had already done.

Very few people refused. The *Informant* paid reasonably well, but that was not the main point. Writing the notes in wordless *Informant* style to games that we had won, penning down the variations in which our luckless opponents might have succumbed in different ways from what really happened, that was no punishment, and anyway we wanted to be represented in the *Informant* because everybody read it.

In July 2010 Krnic, a mild-mannered and friendly man, was hit by a motorcyclist at a crossroads and died a week later, without having regained consciousness, in a Beograd hospital. I had long stopped contributing to the *Informants* for lack of decent games to show, but I will miss his presence.

Bombshells by Velimirovic

1000 TN!! starts with a list of winners, those whom the jury had selected at least once as originators of the best novelty of the previous *Informant*. Anand heads the list with nine top novelties. Karpov, never keen on opening study but in charge of a highly competent staff, won eight times, Kasparov and Kramnik five times and Velimirovic and Topalov four times.

Younger chess fans may be surprised by the presence of Dragoljub Velimirovic among five World Champions, but those who followed him in the 70's remember his deadly hammer blows in the openings very well.

Here is one of them.

Dragoljub Velimirovic
RK Al Kazzaz
Nice Olympiad 1974

1.e4 c5 2.♘f3 d6 3.d4 cxd4 4.♘xd4 ♘f6 5.♘c3 a6 6.♗g5 e6 7.f4 ♗e7 8.♕f3 ♕c7 9.0-0-0 ♘bd7 10.♗d3 b5 11.♖he1 ♗b7 12.♕g3 0-0-0

13.♗xb5 This is an improvement (well, maybe) on 13.♗xf6, as in Spassky-Fischer, 15th match game 1972. Velimirovic's novelty is still alive after almost 40 years; the latest game in my database with 13.♗xb5 is Negi-Sasikiran, Dubai Open 2011, 1-0.
13...axb5 14.♘dxb5 ♕b6 15. e5 d5 16.f5 ♘h5 17.♕h4 ♗xg5+ 18.♕xg5 ♘xe5 19.♕xh5 d4 20.♖xe5 dxc3 21.♘xc3 ♖xd1+ 22.♕xd1 ♖d8 23.♕e1 exf5 24.♖xf5 ♕h6+ 25.♔b1 ♕xh2 26.♖xf7 ♕xg2 27.♕e6+ ♔b8 28.♕e5+ 1-0.

Great work of the Soviet machine
Bobby Fischer is absent on the list of winners. This is not completely surprising, since his active career coincides only for a few years with the period dealt with in this book. There are a few novelties by Fischer in the book that did not win top honours: Fischer-Unzicker, Olympiad Siegen 1970, 10th place in *Informant* 11. Two novelties from his Candidates' match against Petrosian in 1971, third and ninth place in *Informant* 12. Two from the match against Spassky in 1972, sixth and ninth place in *Informant* 14, and one against Spassky

in 1992, eighth place in *Informant* 55.

When comparing Fischer's opening novelties in his 1972 match with Spassky's, we see that against Fischer's two rather low-ranked novelties, Spassky produced five, which gained first, second, fourth, fifth and seventh place on the list of *Informant* 14.

Of course this does not imply that Spassky had worked harder and better on his openings than Fischer. The opposite is almost certainly true. It just serves to illustrate the well-known fact that an army of Soviet analysts had supported Spassky and that they had delivered good work.

Fantastic move, but not eligible
Faced with a cornucopia of beautiful and often striking innovations, only a miserable whiner will complain about the absence of one of his darlings. But I must say that at first I couldn't understand the absence of a move that I, wildly enthusiastic, called the novelty of the century in a newspaper report immediately after it had been played.

Ivanchuk-Shirov
Wijk aan Zee 1996
position after 20...♖d7

21.♕g7
What a move! When you see it, you understand it, as White gets two pieces and a mighty pawn on g7 for his queen. It is so brilliant that in Wijk aan Zee I briefly thought of a computer error. Later it was established that, objectively speaking, Black is not so bad, but Ivanchuk went on to win a fine game.

Why was this marvel not on the list in *Informant* 65? Number one there was Adams-Dreev, also from Wijk aan Zee 1996, which indeed had a strong and important novelty in a topical sacrificial variation of the French. OK, tastes may differ, I thought, but I still couldn't comprehend that Ivanchuk was not on that list at all, not even in 10th place.

Number 10 on that list was the following game, again from Wijk aan Zee.

Alexey Shirov
Jan Timman
Wijk aan Zee 1996
1.e4 e5 2.♘f3 ♘c6 3.♗b5 a6 4. ♗a4 ♘f6 5.0-0 ♘xe4 6.d4 b5 7. ♗b3 d5 8.dxe5 ♗e6 9.♘bd2 ♘c5 10.c3 d4

11.♘g5

This amazing move, first played in Karpov-Kortchnoi 1978, 10th match game, was the deserving winner on the list of *Informant* 26. As every Russian schoolboy knows, it was actually thought up by Karpov's second Igor Zaitsev. It would be nice to know which of all these 1000 novelties were invented by the player himself and which by a 'genius in the background', but of course this is impossible.

11...♕xg5 12.♕f3 0-0-0 13. ♗xe6+ fxe6 14.♕xc6 ♕xe5 15. b4 ♕d5 16.♕xd5 exd5 17.bxc5 dxc3 18.♘b3 d4 19.♗a3

19...g6 This was Timman's novelty compared to Timman-Smyslov 1979, where Smyslov had played 19...♗e7. At first I thought that replacing the manoeuvre ...♗f8-e7-f6 with ...g6 and ...♗g7 was not so earth-shaking as to merit a special distinction, but I was wrong. There is more here than immediately meets the eye.

20.♗b4 ♗g7 21.a4 ♔d7 22.axb5 axb5 23.♖ad1

In his book *Fire on Board* Shirov explains the idea behind Timman's novelty. In Timman-Smyslov, with Black's bishop on f6, White played 23.♖a6, with the idea of 23...♖a8 24.♖xf6 gxf6 25.♘xd4. Here 23.♖a6 would be pointless after 23...♖a8. Subtle indeed. Timman's novelty gave him a more or less equal game, but he still lost.

23...♔e6 24.♖fe1+ ♔d5 25.♗xc3 ♔c4 26.♗a5 ♔xb3 27.♖b1+ ♔c4 28.♖ec1+ ♔d5 29.c6 ♔d6 30.♖xb5 ♖b8 31.♗b4+ ♔e6 32.♖e1+ ♔f6 33.♗e7+ ♔f7 34.♖d5 ♖hc8 35.♖d7 ♔g8 36.g3 ♖b6 37.♖c1 ♖b3 38. ♗c5 d3 39.♖d1 ♖cb8 40.♔g2 ♗f8

41.♗xf8 ♖xf8 42.♖1xd3 ♖xd3 43. ♖xd3 ♖f7 44.f4 ♔e7 45.g4 ♖e6 46. ♖d8+ ♔f7 47.♖d7+ ♔e7 48.♖xe7+ ♔xe7 49.g5 1-0.

I'll return to this position later, but first let's go back to Ivanchuk's game. Consulting a database, I finally realized that his wonderful 21.♕g7 had not been in contention for top honours or any honour at all because of a formality. The first new move in Ivanchuk-Shirov had not been 21.♕g7 but 20... ♖d7, where 20...♔b8 had been played earlier. What a pity. I think the editors should have bent the rules a bit in this case.

Browsing through these novelties evokes many pleasant memories of wonderful chess.

A sad memory for Dutch patriots is connected with the final position of Shirov-Timman. *1000 TN!!* contains a note by Shirov which explains Timman's resignation with the line (among others) 49...♔d6 50.h4 ♔xc6 51.f5 ♔d6 52.f6, winning. This must have been Shirov's original note.

But in *Fire on Board* he recognizes that the position after 52.f6 is actually a draw, because White cannot win pawn c7, and that Timman had resigned in a drawn position. Timman himself, with good reason, called it the worst blunder of the tournament.

Barge haulers on the Volga

On Vladislav Tkachiev's website *WhyChess*, which had a flying start and a short life, Alexander Grischuk once referred to a report that had originally appeared in *The Guardian*, about prisoners in a Chinese labour camp who were forced to play computer games such as *World of Warcraft*, day and night. They had to gain credits that the prison administration then sold to wealthy customers to enable them to enter the game at a higher level by means of the credits earned by the prisoners, who were beaten with plastic pipes when they had not fulfilled their quota of credits.

The comparison with chess seconds, working at the computer day and night to invent novelties for their masters, comes naturally, although Grischuk did not make it explicitly.

The frantic concentration on openings has often been deplored, also by those who are compelled to take part in it. Vladimir Kramnik has spoken about the drudgery of sifting through the thousands of games that *The Week in Chess* supplies every week. Sergey Shipov once made a comparison between Russian players and the barge haulers on the Volga, depicted by the painter Ilya Repin. Fischer made fun of the thick glasses worn by modern top players who had been wearing their eyes out at the computer screen.

Apart from the fact that it is probably a myth that eyes can deteriorate by being strained, I think that most top players would gladly upgrade their glasses for an important novelty.

It's true that the hunt for novelties, at home, at the computer desk, takes a lot away from the spontaneity of the battle at the board. But there is another side to it. It may be worth it.

Going through *1000 TN!!* you see a wealth of brilliant inventions and fine games resulting from them. You see a world in motion, continually enriched by new and often spectacular ideas. Would we want to be without all these home-made novelties for the sake of spontaneity at the board? Chess would soon become boring, I think. Fischerandom is nice for a change, but it cannot replace the game that we have. Anyway, this book is a monument to creativity in a guided tour of the best of chess in more than 40 years. ∎

The adrenaline lover

VLADIMIR BARSKY

Valentina Gunina at a junior training session. 'Valya stood out for her liveliness and spontaneity: it seemed that she just couldn't ever be in a bad mood.'

With a nerve-wrecking last-round win over her closest rival, Valentina Gunina won the European Women's Championship in Gaziantep, Turkey, edging out Tatiana Kosintseva and Anna Muzychuk on a better tie-break. **Vladimir Barsky** meets with the new European (and current Russian!) champion in Moscow, where she lives these days. Lively and spontaneous as always, the 23-year-old 'Tal in a skirt' talks openly about her youth in distant Murmansk, the sacrifices she and her family had to make, her ambitions, the hardships of professional chess life and the adrenaline that makes it all worth it.

I first met Valya Gunina in the summer of 2004 at a training session that grandmaster and coach Sergey Yanovsky had organized for the strongest Russian juniors. The kids were a great mix – Ian Nepomniachtchi, Zhenya Tomashevsky, Ildar Khairullin, Sasha Kharitonov; the girls, besides Valya, were Nastya Savina and Lena Tairova, who left us too soon. The chief instructor was Mark Dvoretsky, and I and two other coaches helped him run the practical lessons, when in the second half we divided the kids into groups of two to three people. Valya stood out for her liveliness and spontaneity: it seemed that she just couldn't ever be in a bad mood – at any moment

she was ready to burst out laughing joyfully and infectiously. She was one of the first to answer chess questions – she often 'didn't guess' the solution (although she never suggested silly moves), but it was clear that she couldn't wait to give an answer. Her reactions were excellent, and she played blitz superbly already at 15.

By the way, Tomashevsky amazed me in those sessions: often when he saw a position on the board he simply named the players and the year when the game was played. For his truly encyclopaedic knowledge his friends started respectfully calling him 'Professor'. Valya, though, turned out to be the complete opposite of him – sometimes you got the impression that she didn't burden herself with any chess knowledge at all. But she was distinguished by her colos-

> 'She only looked at the enemy king, easily parting with pawns and pieces if only she could create an attack.'

sal effort, her fearlessness, her excellent calculating, her staying-power – for the time being all this compensated for the obvious gaps in her classical education.

Valya is from Murmansk, a port city in the far north of the Kola Peninsula, relatively close to the border with Norway and Finland. Thanks to the Gulf Stream the winters there aren't too severe, but there are very strong winds, and Valya recalls that she almost got blown away once when she was little. In summer the temperature rarely goes above +20, so you can only sunbathe on your balcony. In other words, it's no holiday resort!

Chess has never been held in particularly high esteem in Murmansk, and how this bright star managed to come out of there is a big question. Although in the neighbouring and also far from chess-loving Norway in the same years a wunderkind by the name of Magnus was growing up; we

have no idea where and when these natural talents appear!

Valya's mother was an accountant, and her father taught advanced maths at a university. Her grandfather, a mechanical engineer who repaired ships, loved chess. A pure amateur, he was able to pass his enthusiasm onto his son, Valya's father, who decided at some point to re-qualify as a chess coach. His eight-year-old son and five-year-old daughter were among his first pupils. But it would be an artificial exaggeration to say that on seeing the chequered board and pieces Valya was immediately fired up with passion for the 'wise and ancient game'.

Gunina recalls: 'At first I didn't like studying it very much, but dad forced me to. Then my brother started getting good, he won the bronze for his age group in the Russian Championship (Grachev was first at the time). But then he lost interest, and I, by contrast, started climbing the mountain.'
So what did you like about chess?
'The adrenaline is a kind of drug! If you don't go anywhere for a month it already starts to get boring.'
You like to travel?
'Yes, to see new places. And that's how I differed from other children. At school everything was monotonous: the subjects, the lessons, the rules; boring daily life... I liked being different somehow. A chess player has a completely different life! But, true, it's very hard – the constant travelling, dragging an unwieldy suitcase on the metro...'

Thanks to her natural talent Valya quickly achieved successes: at the age of nine she won the Under-10 Russian Championship, and she constantly took medals in championships of the country, Europe and the world. But she slowed down at about 14-15, and the reason turned out to be banal – the lack of a strong coach. Her father tried very hard, of course, but he didn't have enough knowledge or pure chess strength. And there was a 'deficit' of good coaches in Murmansk.

In those years I was coaching Ildar Khairullin, travelling with him to important tournaments and studying the games of his male peers rather carefully, and those of his female peers at the same time. Valya Gunina, as I saw it, played in a 'kick and rush' style: she only looked at the enemy king, easily parting with pawns and pieces if only she could create an attack. She was 'Tal in a skirt' (although, to be honest, I don't remember if she often wore a skirt or a dress; I think jeans were and remain the basis of her wardrobe). Her young female opponents often got confused by this kind of pressure, but the more experienced ones willingly accepted the sacrifices and just smacked their lips. To me this seems to be a typical episode.

Gunina-Stepovaia
Sochi 2004
position after 17...h5

White unpretentiously played the Dutch Defence, trying to get far away from theory as fast as she could. Castling long indicates a desire to get a sharper position. Now there's approximate equality on the board: White has to remember her weak c5 pawn and Black her rather exposed king. It probably made sense for White to undertake a regrouping – change the places of the knight and queen to defend the c5 pawn and get the g6 pawn in her sights. But Gunina only looks forward!
18.♖h3 ♔h7 19.f3 ♖ae8
The very experienced Tatiana Stepovaia herself also very much likes to attack, but her arsenal of technical methods was much richer at the time

than the young Valya's. Two accurate prophylactic moves – and what should White do now?

20.♖hh1
The bugler blows the last post. Having convinced herself that playing g2-g4 was unrealistic and that boldly sacrificing her rook somehow on g6 was unlikely to work either, Valya decides to move her rook closer to the centre. A minimum of two tempi lost.
20...♕e7 And how to save the c5 pawn now? Gunina sets a little trap.
21.♔b1

21...♗d7
On 21...♕xc5, obviously, 22.♘xe6 ♖xe6 23.♗xf5 would follow. True, if she doesn't take the bishop but just moves the rook away, Black is a little better here too. But Stepovaia, of course, easily avoids the simple trap. Losing the pawn is inevitable now. White's best chance was possibly a blow in the centre: 22.e4 fxe4 23.fxe4 ♕xc5 24.exd5 cxd5, and after 25.♘b3 ♕c7 26.♘d4 she can defend stubbornly. But Valechka likes to attack energetically, not 'defend stubbornly'!
22.♗xf5!? gxf5 23.♘xf5 ♗xf5 24.♕xf5+ ♔h8 25.e4 dxe4

VLADIMIR BARSKY

Valentina Gunina, holding the stuffed tiger that became the mascotte of the Russian team, and Tatiana Kosintseva at the Khanty-Mansiysk Olympiad.

26.f4 It's on this zwischenzug that White's idea was built. After 26...♘f7 27.♕xh5+ (but just not 27.♖d7? ♘h6!) 27...♔g7 28.♕g4+ she hardly risks losing, and there may even be a chance to mate the black king. In a junior tournament no one would have been surprised by White winning. But you can't surprise Stepovaia with these kinds of tricks.

26...♕h7!
The last accurate move, after which the battle, in essence, ends. Black gives the piece back but forces a transfer

into a technical endgame a pawn up.
27.♕xh7+ ♔xh7 28.fxe5 ♖xe5 29.♖d7+ ♔g6 30.♖e1 f5 31.♖a7 a4 32.b3 axb3 33.axb3 ♖xc5
and a dozen or so moves later Black made good on her advantage.

Valya Gunina tells the story: 'I studied books with my dad, he was always giving me positions to solve. But that isn't quite it; I studied a lot, but sometimes in a vacuum. Of course, there was some benefit, otherwise I wouldn't have improved at all, but I kind of improved 'on the side'. True, on my trips to Europe and the rest of the world I worked with Sergey Moiseevich Yanovsky. In the evenings we got together and demonstrated our games – it was very interesting to listen to Zhenya Tomashevsky and Ian Nepomniachtchi. In the mornings Yanovsky prepared those of us who didn't have a personal coach. But there were a lot of us, and he was one person for the whole delegation. Sometimes he prepared two people at once... He did organize the first training sessions for me (the same ones with which our story began – V.B.), and after them I won the Under-16 World Championship. And immediately things went uphill, I was noticed.'
You had no problem travelling to tournaments?
'Every time, dad and I had to go and ask permission. At the local sport

committee they said that for them the main types of sport were skiing, biathlon and boxing, but not chess. So if I didn't win a medal at the world or European then I wouldn't go anywhere any more. Very harsh condi-

> 'He explained that it's better to use up all your time and find the best move than to play quickly but superficially.'

tions, which is why I always had to win something!'

Did your dad pay for his own travel with you?

'Yes, and we had to economize terribly on everything – on food, for example, and living somewhere illegally.'

There were rumours that he virtually slept under a palm tree!

'Yes, because a hotel room is expensive. But he usually managed to find someone to stay with. At least it was good that as my coach they started paying dad something for my wins.'

When you finished school had you already decided to become a chess player?

'I went to school very little, so I had to choose between two chess departments in Moscow. In the end I enrolled at RSSU [the Russian State Social University] (Karjakin, Nepomniachtchi and other well-known chess players study at this institution, and the biggest open tournament in Russia takes place within its walls – V.B.). In the

capital there are far more opportunities for improvement, you can simply, for example, go into the Central Chess Club and play whenever you want.'

Have coaches finally appeared in Moscow?

'Yes. If you are enrolled at RSSU and studying in the Anatoly Karpov School, you don't pay for coaching. I have two coaches at the moment – grandmaster Alexander Kalinin and international master Igor Yanvarev.'

After that you had a qualitative leap?

'Of course! And then RSSU set up two training sessions for me with grandmaster Alexey Korotylev, and I realized that I'd been doing everything wrong at home. The strain was horrible, I thought that I wouldn't be able to stand it.'

Korotylev tormented you?

'I played very quickly at that time, and he gave me a task and set the clocks for 15-20 minutes. I wasn't allowed to make a move until all the time had run out. But my hands were itching terribly, I wanted to move immediately. Korotylev set a tough condition: I always had to use all my thinking time. I was tormented for a whole week, and then I trained myself, and even at tournaments there wasn't enough time for me any more, I started getting into time trouble. But now I've adapted somehow.'

Did Alexey help you to look at chess differently?

'He taught me diligence. He explained that it's better to use up all your time and find the best move than to play quickly but superficially. I had been playing instantaneously. That's good for blitz, of course, but not for classical chess. I managed to improve noticeably because I learned to think seriously about my moves.'

I remember the energetic attacks you launched!

'I have that kind of personality – it's all or nothing! I can throw in all my pieces and start attacking my opponent. Now I try to act more carefully, but still, sometimes you're in the mood for accurate play, then as soon

as a commotion begins you forget everything else in the world!'

When did you manage to get into the Super Final for the first time?

'I was still at school. Obviously with that kind of preparation there was nothing I could do there. It took me five years to get into the top three.'

Didn't you do really badly in your first three Super Finals?

'Yes, I got five or six zeroes. My opening preparation was weak, and I wasn't diligent enough. Even if I got decent positions I was outplayed. No experience, no class – nothing.'

What did getting onto the team teach you?

'When you get on the team the prizes are very big. You no longer have to play in everything to earn enough money for food. I could then choose my tournaments. At the training sessions I worked with Kobalia and Korotylev, and recently Rublevsky came to us. Two training sessions a year before the biggest events – at minimum. And the day-to-day support also has an effect.'

Did Dokhoian also work with you?

'Yury Rafaelovich helped the Kosintseva sisters more. But when you go to a team meeting he always explains to you where you made a mistake. He said lots of interesting things about his work with Kasparov. He drew our attention to the psychological nuances. Well, and his strictness helped us, of course. And if the game doesn't go well, he talks to you from his heart, and it becomes easier.

'I really like being on our team. The girls are very sociable. If something happens to you, they always help. We have fun in our free time. Naturally, Dokhoian arranged things so that we work hard first, and if we win, then we can have a good time. And we all work very hard to win!'

At the 2010 Olympiad in Khanty-Mansiysk Gunina brought our team quite a few important points. For example, it was to her that a queen was blundered in the extremely important match with China. So Valya is lucky, too! Perhaps it was all due to the stuffed tiger that Valya always had with her? It became the favourite mascot of the team that won – so nice to remember! – all 11 matches.

A year later Valya became the Russian women's champion, getting past her friends from the team in a tough Super Final. But she might not have gone to the European Championship that she won at all. The organization where Gunina works as a player-instructor promised to pay for her trip, but either due to intrigue or plain old sloppiness the money for the trip never materialized. She didn't have any spare resources: it had all gone on repairs to the flat she had recently purchased just outside Moscow. (In Valya's words, after four and a half years she was totally fed up of living in a dormitory and after saving her money she immediately bought a home for herself.) Fortunately generous people helped her.

Valya Gunina tells the story:
'After the agitation before the start it was hard to play at first. I was apparently in good form, I could calculate variations, but I wasn't composed enough. Of course, there wasn't even any question of my coach travelling with me. I had to communicate with Kalinin via Skype. Plus the internet turned out to be very slow, we weren't able to talk, and we had to type. He typed the text of the key games and I put them on the computer and looked at them. And then many of the players started getting sick...

'Although, the organizers tried hard, they created decent conditions overall. But we weren't very lucky with the weather either, and the food was always the same.'
Good or not very?
'Good, but after three weeks I managed to get tired of it. And everyone started getting sick: someone had a nosebleed, someone else had something else. I had a strange condition – I got tired very quickly. But then my confidence started coming back. Up until the end I didn't think that it

There is a reason for the saying 'No one's lucky like a first prize-winner'! Antoaneta Stefanova lent the new European Champion a helping hand when she totally lost control in a winning position.

would all turn out so well, but I was just in a very bad mood!'
Why?
'Because they didn't give me the money, as usual, it's all decided in one place...'
Were you angry at the whole world?
'Yes. Usually when I'm angry it helps.'

If we only judge by the points she scored, Valya started very confidently – four out of five. But in the sixth round she was outplayed on all fronts by ex-world champion Antoaneta Stefanova.

Stefanova-Gunina
Gaziantep 2012 (6)
position after 23...a5

White is starting to look like she's three pawns up ☺. There is also a forced win – apparently a straightforward one: 24.♘f4 ♖xd4 25.♘e6! But here something incomprehensible begins.
24.e6?! ♖f5 25.♕d6 fxe6

26.♘g3 White's position still remained winning, but why not hide the king – 26.♕xe6+ ♔h8 27.0-0, as on 27...♖e8 the move 28.♕d7 is easily found, with the threat of mate.
26...♖5f6 27.♘h5 ♖6f7 28.♖xf7 ♖xf7 29.♔d2

The king is still in the centre – a small reason for Black to be happy! And White is now only two pawns up.
29...♗f5 30.♖c1 a4 31.b4 ♕e8 32.♘g3 ♖d7 33.♕f4 ♗g6 34.♖c5 ♕d8 35.♔e3 h6 36.♘e2 a3

Gunina 'scrambles for her life' with all her might: White now has to worry about the a2 pawn.
37.♕e5 ♗b1 38.♘c3 ♗f5 39.g4 ♗g6 40.♘e4 ♔h7 41.g5

Here or earlier White could have just pushed the b-pawn to queen. But you get the impression that Stefanova wanted a definite checkmate.
41...h5 42.h4 ♕b6 43.♖b5 ♕a6 44.♕b8 ♖f7 45.♘d2 ♕a4
Gunina patiently searches for breaches through which her pieces could 'percolate' towards the enemy camp.
46.♘b3

46...♖f8! In the case of an exchange of rooks it wouldn't be easy for White to defend her rear, as her king has no refuge anywhere. The computer, of course, easily gets around all the obstacles, but a person in this situation inevitably starts to get annoyed. Two pawns up but a direct win isn't evident, and what's worse – she has to be careful all the time!
47.♕b7 ♖f7 48.♕b8 ♖f8 49.♕b6 ♕a8 50.♕b7 ♕d8 51.♕c6 ♗e8 52.♕c2+ ♗g6 53.♕c3 ♕e7

Black has clearly manoeuvred more successfully than her opponent. Her forces are coordinated and her king is solidly covered. But White has moved her pieces somewhere off to the left, her pawns are immobile and her king is misplaced. Stefanova should have restructured accurately and returned her pieces to the centre, but instead of that a blunder followed.
54.♔e2?

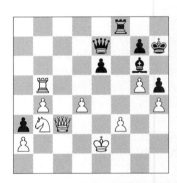

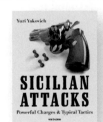

54...♖f4! It seems the chances have now equalized.

55.♙b8 ♖xh4 56.♕c8

White is again looking for a mate, but she herself comes under attack.

56...♖h2+ 57.♔e1 ♗c2 58.♘d2 ♖h1+ 59.♔f2 ♖h2+ 60.♔e1 ♖h1+ 61.♔f2 ♖h2+ 62.♔e1 ♗d3! A courageous decision: Black has spent so much time completely out of the game, she is still a pawn down, but a repetition of moves no longer suits her! And Stefanova can't withstand the strain.

63.f4? 63.♕h8+ ♔g6 64.♖g8! maintained equality, tying Black's queen and king to the g7 pawn. Now, though, Black brings her queen into the attack.

63...♕d6 64.♕g8+ ♔g6 65.♘f3 ♖h1+ 66.♔f2 ♖f1+ 67.♔g2 ♖xf3 67...♕d5 is simpler, but this is more impressive!

68.♔xf3 ♕d5+

69.♔g3 Here's the 'strong' variation: 69.♔e3 ♕e4+ 70.♔d2 ♕e2+ 71.♔c3 ♕c2 mate.

69...h4+ 70.♔xh4 ♕h1+ 71.♔g3 ♕e1+ 72.♔h3 ♗f5+ 73.♔g2 ♗e4+ 74.♔h3 ♕h1+ 75.♔g3 ♕g2+ 76.♔h4 ♕f2+ 77.♔h3 ♗f5 Mate.

There's a reason for the saying 'No one's lucky like a first prize-winner'! After this gift from fate Gunina with five points came out in second place, remaining half a point behind the leader – Hoang Thanh Trang. Then there was a rest day in the tournament, and after it Valya routed a Hungarian player and came out on the top line, but not alone, sharing it with Foisor. Then Gunina slowed down and made three draws in a row, while Anna Muzychuk from Slovenia won three games and first caught up with the leaders, then broke away and before the final, eleventh round, was ahead of Gunina and Tatiana Kosintseva by a whole point.

NOTES BY
Valentina Gunina

SL 6.9 – D43
Valentina Gunina
Anna Muzychuk
Gaziantep 2012 (11)

This game took place in the last round. Anna was the sole leader, a point ahead of me. Of course, I very much wanted to win, but it was even more important not to lose!

I think that from the psychological point of view it was easier for me, because Anna had to play a second successive game with black. Before the game the arbiters posted up the participants' positions, and it became clear to me that, in the event of a share of first place, the tie-break would most probably be better for me.

I played the game quite calmly, thinking that if I did not manage to win it would not be anything terrible. My trainer encouraged me in the same way, saying that the main thing was not to overstep the mark!

1.d4 d5 2.c4 c6 3.♘f3 ♘f6 4.♘c3 e6 5.♗g5 h6 6.♗xf6

In accordance with the chosen strategy. Of course, the Moscow Variation is not the sharpest opening. Although

---

I also had some ideas in the Anti-Moscow Gambit, I decided not to burn my boats.

6...♕xf6 7.e3 ♘d7

In the European Championship I had already played two games with the Moscow Variation, in which I scored 1½ points.

8.♗d3

In the second round I chose 8.♗e2, and the position turned out roughly equal, but later I nevertheless outplayed a rather inexperienced opponent.

8...dxc4 9.♗xc4 g6 10.0-0 ♗g7

11.♖e1

This move was shown to me by Kolya Chadaev. In previous games I had unsuccessfully tried to implement an idea which he had explained to me.

The main continuation here is 11.♖c1, and after 11...0-0 12.e4 e5 13.d5 ♘b6 14.♗b3 ♗g4 Black exchanges on f3, breaking up White's kingside pawns. This, for example, is how my game went against Wang Yu in the Russia-China match, Ningbo 2010. After 15.h3 ♗xf3 16.♕xf3 ♕xf3 17.gxf3

ANALYSIS DIAGRAM

an endgame slightly better for White was reached. I managed to win it, but I realized that against Anna this was unlikely to happen. Of course, she has more opening knowledge, since I don't greatly enjoy working on the opening.

11...0-0 12.e4 e5 13.d5 ♖d8

But all my plans were disrupted by this move, which my opponent made very quickly. Naturally, I did not remember anything apart from the idea of ♖e3, and I had to start thinking for myself. If 13...♘b6 the plan was 14.♗b3 ♗g4 15.♖e3, in order to reply to ...♗xf3 by capturing with the rook and not allowing the break-up of the pawn chain.

14.♖e3

14...b5?!

I thought for a long time what I would do in the event of 14...♘b6 15.♗b3 cxd5 16.♘xd5 ♘xd5 17.♗xd5 ♗e6, since here White's advantage is altogether minimal. I was also concerned about 15...♗e6 (instead of 15...cxd5) 16.♖d3 cxd5 17.♘xd5 (also nothing is given by 17.exd5 ♗f5) 17...♘xd5 18.♗xd5 ♗xd5 19.♖xd5 ♖xd5

20.♕xd5 ♕b6, when the position is close to equal, and after 21.♘xe5 ♕xb2 22.♕xf7+ ♔h7 23.♕xg6+ ♔g8 White is obliged to force a draw by perpetual check.

I calculated all these variations during the game. True, there is also the possibility of playing 15.♕b3 and maintaining some tension. It is probable that, as long as the g7-bishop has not switched to another diagonal, White should be a little better. But Anna quickly made the move in the game.

15.dxc6

If the bishop retreats there follows 15...b4 and then 16...cxd5, when White has no convenient recapture on d5.

15...bxc4

16.♘d5!

I think that Anna overlooked this intermediate move. Here she thought for a long time. Of course, 16.cxd7 and then 17.♘d5 was possible, but then Black has more choice; for example, she can play her queen to a6.

16...♕d6

I mainly studied 16...♕e6 with the idea of indirectly defending the c4-pawn. But then in reply to 17.cxd7 Black has to take with the rook, to avoid the fork on c7. Even so, in my view the move in the game is weaker: at d6 the queen will be 'hanging', and Black will have to spend another tempo moving it to a more appropriate post.

17.cxd7 ♗xd7 18.♘d2

Here my position already very much appealed to me. In addition, I noticed that Anna had become nervous, since the c4-pawn can easily be lost. And yet Black only needed a draw!

18...♗b5 Perhaps my opponent had been counting on 18...♗c6, but after 19.♘xc4 ♕c5 20.♖c1 ♗xd5 21. ♖d3 White will be a sound pawn to the good. Black has to defend the c4-pawn with the bishop.

19.♕c2 ♖ab8 20.♖c3

My rook on the 3rd rank is getting through quite a lot of work, while the other rook is covering the back rank.

20...♕a6 21.a4 ♗f8

At this point I thought for a long time. And indeed, what should be done? The dark-squared bishop is planning to switch to its required diagonal, and the light-squared bishop cannot be taken, since the rook is hanging. My time began dwindling at an alarming rate.

22.♘f1

I also calculated 22.♘xc4 ♗xc4 23. ♖xc4 ♖xb2 24.♕xb2 ♕xc4, when 25.♖d1 ♕xe4 26.♘f6+ ♔g7 is bad – White is let down by the weakness of the back rank.

Here 22.♘c7 is very interesting, but then 22...♕d6 23.♘xb5?! ♕xd2 24.♕xd2 ♖xd2 25.♖xc4 a6, and the advantage is with Black. I calculated 23.♘xc4 ♗xc4 24.♖xc4 as well, but just in time I saw 24...♖xb2!, when

The decisive game. Valentina Gunina defeated Anna Muzychuk to catch up with her and take the title on tie-break.

Black wins. But after 23.axb5 ♕xc7 the b5-pawn is just as weak as the c4-pawn, and therefore the chances are equal. Of course, it is possible to bring the knight back – 23.♘d5, to which Black replies 23...♕a6, and the position is repeated.

In the end I decided to play my knight to e3, where it will obviously be better placed than on d2, supporting its colleague on d5. And I also managed to guess my opponent's reply.

22...♗c5?! It was this move that I calculated most of all. But 22...♗c6 was correct: after 23.♘fe3 White's position is somewhat more pleasant, but, I think, not by much.

23.♕c1!

Attacking the h6-pawn and at the same time defending the rook on a1.

23...♗c6 It was precisely this variation that I was aiming for.

24.♘f6+ True, I slightly miscalculated. Initially here I had been planning 24.♕xh6 and I thought that I would gain a terrifying attack, but I noticed in time that after 24...♗xd5 25.♖h3 there is the queen move 25...♕f6 – Black defends everything and obtains a big advantage.

24...♔g7 25.♘g4

Now Black has an unpleasant position, and I am able to combine threats on both wings.

25...g5 The times began to even up. I sensed that Anna was very nervous.

26.♖xc4 Both Black's bishops are hanging, but she finds a latent resource.

Gaziantep 2012

					TPR
1	Valentina Gunina	IM	2511	8½	2660
2	Tatiana Kosintseva	IGM	2513	8½	2649
3	Anna Muzychuk	IGM	2583	8½	2631
4	Victoria Cmilyte	IGM	2497	8	2592
5	Marie Sebag	IGM	2512	7½	2570
6	Antoaneta Stefanova	IGM	2531	7½	2544
7	Kateryna Lahno	IGM	2546	7½	2524
8	Elina Danielian	IGM	2478	7½	2515
9	Bela Khotenashvili	IM	2490	7½	2503
10	Natalija Pogonina	WM	2449	7½	2501
11	Alexandra Kosteniuk	IGM	2448	7½	2437
12	Hoang Thanh Trang	IGM	2438	7	2510
13	Nino Khurtsidze	IM	2447	7	2505
14	Nana Dzagnidze	IGM	2559	7	2468
15	Salome Melia	IM	2400	7	2461
16	Baira Kovanova	WM	2392	7	2452
17	Lela Javakhishvili	IM	2448	7	2450
18	Marina Romanko	IM	2417	7	2444
19	Anna Ushenina	IM	2458	7	2429
20	Natalia Zhukova	IGM	2435	7	2415
21	Nadezhda Kosintseva	IGM	2535	7	2406
22	Cristina-Adela Foisor	IM	2398	6½	2509
23	Zoya Schleining	WM	2326	6½	2483
24	Olga Girya	WM	2406	6½	2448
	103 players, 11 rounds				

26...♖d1! And the game continues.
27.♕xd1 ♕xc4 28.♕f3

After the game GM Evgeny Miroshnichenko, who was commenting for the spectators, told me that the computer recommended 28.♘g3, when the capture 28...♗xe4? is not possible on account of 29.♖c1 or 29.♕e1!.

28...♕xe4

If 28...♕e6 I would have continued carrying out my plan with 29.♘g3.

29.♖c1!

But not 29.♕f6+ because of 29...♔g8 – again mate is threatened, and White does not manage to do anything.

From the reaction of my opponent I realized that my last move had come as an unpleasant surprise to her.

29...♕g6

I also studied 29...f5 30.♘xe5 ♕xe5 31.♕xc6 – White is a pawn up, but the main thing is that the enemy king is totally exposed.

30.♕c3 ♕e4

The ♕e4-g6-e4 manoeuvre somewhat surprised me, and it was only later than I understood Black's idea.

31.♕xe5+ ♕xe5 32.♘xe5 ♗xf2+ 33.♔xf2 ♖xb2+ 34.♔e3 ♗xg2 35.♘g3

From my opponent's face I realized that she was expecting 35.♖c7, after which I did not like the reply 35...♔f6. Although in fact after 36.♘d2! White retains all the advantages of her position.

35...♗d5

The variation I liked least was 35...♔f6 36.♘g4+ ♔e6 37.♘xh6. The black king moves out of the mating net, and my knights become rather unwieldy. And White has only two pawns left – there may not be enough material for a win.

36.♘h5+

White takes the opportunity to encage the enemy king. True, 36.♖c7 was also not bad.

36...♔f8 37.♖d1

37...♗e6?? Possibly Black should have defended by 37...♖xh2 38.♖d5 ♖xh5, but I thought that after 39.♖d7 White had a big advantage.

I also didn't like the move 37...♖b3+. After 38.♔d4 ♗e6 I can no longer invade the enemy position with my rook. If 38.♖d3, then 38...♖xd3+ 39.♔xd3 ♔e7, and here I am not sure that White can convert her advantage. I also studied 38.♔f2 ♖b2+ 39.♔g1 (of course, in the endgame White does not greatly want to move the king away from the centre) 39...♖g2+ 40.♔f1 ♖xh2 41.♖xd5 ♖xh5 42.♖a5, but I don't know whether or not White has a win here.

But when Anna lost a piece she began playing somehow as though doomed, and she overlooked a mate in two.

38.♖d8+ Black resigned.

■ ■ ■

Tanya Kosintseva beat Nana Dzagnidze as Black and joined in sharing 1st-3rd place. According to the additional indices Valya took gold and Tanya silver. Let's continue our conversation with the champion.

'After the classical chess you decided to stay and continue the battle in the rapid and blitz championships.'

'I stayed because my home was being renovated. That was the main reason. Besides that, I really like rapid and blitz chess, because there's a lot of adrenaline in it. That's why I like roller-coasters: when everything is going past quickly, the scenery is changing non-stop, you get a ton of pleasure! But, naturally, in speed play you also use up a lot of nerves. In the rapid I finished ninth, that day I wasn't seeing anything at all.

Then came a rest day and the blitz. We played two games in each round – as White and as Black. I won four, then lost four – to Zhukova and Ushenina. And I realized that I wasn't seeing anything, I was blundering everything! Zhukova simply outplayed me. I was so angry! I got to my room and almost started swearing! But then I calmed down and stopped trying to "get my own back". After my loss to Zhukova I decided to "get my own back", although my coach always told me that such efforts never lead to anything good. I calmed down and started to enjoy playing. And somehow things happened by themselves and I started winning everything, except with Pähtz we were 1-1. In the last round I had to win two games "to order" against Stefanova. And it happened, I even caught her queen in the centre of the board as Black!'

Where did you go on the rest day?

'To the fortress, the market, the mosaic museum. They have digital screens there that you can touch to put mosaics together. They told us about the history of the region, about Alexander the Great. I liked it.'

What did you buy at the market?

'I walked around, I browsed. The silver there is very pure and cheap, you can find very interesting hand-crafted things. On the other rest day I went to a shopping centre: they have the same things that are sold in Moscow, only they're two or three times cheaper. They

are brought to us from Turkey, so some of the girls filled whole suitcases – whoever could afford it.

'The big advantage of life in Moscow is that it's much easier to get home. We returned tired after two transfers, not having slept enough, as we had to get up at five in the morning. And it was much easier for those of us who lived in Moscow. I took a taxi and went home, where my mum was already waiting with dinner! But if I'd lived in the provinces I would still have had to wait for a train. At midnight. And if you fly into Moscow late, you spend the night in the airport or at the train station, because hotels are expensive.

'It's good that Yanovsky took care of us: he fed us at his house and helped us find somewhere to stay. It was hard then, we didn't have much money... They gave us a per diem of 60 to 100 roubles, which is just a joke. So we spent the night at stations. I already had my technique worked out: how to lie down, how to stretch my legs out. Dad and I took turns watching the suitcases, but mainly, of course, I slept and he kept a lookout. Then another whole day waiting for a train, and 38 hours jolting along, often hungry... Sometimes the glass in the compartment was broken, there was cardboard instead, and the wind blew unbelievably. Once I got a really bad cold, with serious consequences... Of course, I know people who even spend four days travelling to Moscow, but still – 38 hours is very hard!'

Valya, tell us as a professional sportsperson: how many women in the world can make a living playing chess? Ten, twenty?

'I think that any kind of sport is extremely selective. You need a multitude of different qualities. Above all, health. A small sprinkling of talent, as not everyone is given that. And, naturally, the ability to work. When I started working with coaches I realized that I could work eight hours a day. You need diligence.

'The profession of chess player is very difficult. You're always living out of suitcases. I don't know how people have families, as they're always on trips. Chess players are special people. We probably belong to the same group as writers and artists. For example, my mum says that I don't listen to anything the first time, and I might not even listen the twentieth time. Chess players are very vulnerable, each of us has our "bugbears". Even at the European I hardly hung out with the other girls because everyone was sitting in their rooms working, each in their own "shell". We crawled out of there only for lunch, dinner and our games. And then we hid again.'

What are your hobbies and interests?

'I love ping-pong! Dad had a table in his club. True, it's not very good for your eyesight. During the championship I played once and my stress reduced, it became easier. But the second time I played I felt that I wasn't hitting the ball because my eyes were tired and weren't seeing anything. I like reading, especially horror stories by Stephen King, I collect his books. But mum sometimes makes a fuss about it, saying I have to read something else. When there's time I like going to the cinema, especially to horror films – it's the same adrenaline.' ■

Lucid Solutions

Luke McShane

There is one quite well-known chess puzzle which never fails to tickle me. You are given the following position, and told that the white king has fallen off the board. On which square should it be replaced?

Raymond Smullyan
Manchester Guardian, 1957
The white king is invisible. Where is he?

The difficulty, of course, is that Black's king is in check, and it's not at all obvious how the position could possibly be legal, given that Black's rook on b5 obstructs the diagonal which might have allowed the bishop on a4 to get there in the first place. And it turns out that the placement of the white king helps explain the mystery.

Retrograde analysis problems like this one, which focus on what happened *before* the diagram was reached, are a pretty esoteric genre, and apart from being fond of this one, I must admit that I've never paid too much attention to them in the past.

In the last issue of *New In Chess*, one of the books which caught my attention was Amatzia Avni's *The Amazing Chess Adventures of Baron Munchausen*. So I was always going to be curious to look at *The Chess Mysteries of Sherlock Holmes*, written by Raymond Smullyan, the same composer of the old favourite quoted above. The book is actually a re-publication by Dover of a book which was originally published in 1979 by Alfred A. Knopf, New York. A quick look at Smullyan's Wikipedia page tells us that Raymond Smullyan (aged 92) is an American mathematician, concert pianist, logician, Taoist philosopher and magician. Since Smullyan, unlike Baron Munchausen, is a real living person, that's a pretty extraordinary collection of achievements!

Just as the Baron served to make Avni's collection of problems more accessible, Smullyan uses Sherlock Holmes as his protagonist. The famous Victorian detective is, of course, known for his formidable powers of observation and reasoning. The character's popular appeal is as strong as it ever was, and in fact the recent UK television series *Sherlock* brought the sleuth into the 21st century, complete with nicotine patches instead of a pipe, providing me and countless others with some highly addictive viewing earlier this year.

Smullyan introduces Holmes and his sidekick Watson (the narrator) as follows:

'What about a stroll to the chess club?' Holmes remarked one early afternoon. 'Why Holmes!' I cried in amazement. 'I did not know you were a chess enthusiast!' 'Not of the conventional sort,' laughed Holmes, 'I do not have too much interest in chess as a *game* – indeed, I do not have much inclination for games in general.' 'But what is chess, if *not* a game?' I asked in astonishment. Holmes' face grew serious. 'There are occasional chess situations, Watson, which challenge the analytic mind as fully as any which arise in real life. Moreover, I have found them as valuable as any exercises I know in developing those powers of pure deduction so essential to dealing with real-life situations.'

Given the popular assumption (mistaken, in my opinion) that playing chess well demands a particularly rigorous, logical mindset, it is actually quite refreshing to see Smullyan imply otherwise – that Holmes would not find much appeal in the game on that basis alone. Probably the detective's most famous turn of phrase is this: 'When you have eliminated the impossible, whatever remains, *however improbable*, must be the truth.' So Smullyan's Holmes is an expert in retro-analysis problems, cast in the mould of one who reasons with iron logic. Arguably, the Holmes of the original stories had a number of other talents, but then so did Botvinnik.

To get a sense of this book, there's really no substitute for an example, and so here's one I found particularly appealing. One of the nice features of retro-analysis problems seems to be the range of ways of actually posing a question. A missing piece is one way, and indeed Smullyan likes to play with some unusual themes in his puzzles such as pieces of ambiguous colour, or 'monochromatic' games, in which no piece ever moves from a white square to a black square, or vice versa. We are told that this position arose from a monochromatic game, that the white king has made less than fourteen moves. The puzzle is to prove that a promotion has taken place.

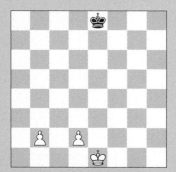

Raymond Smullyan
Chess Mysteries of Sherlock Holmes, page 24

In the first part of the book, the solutions are interspersed with the problems themselves, so if you get stuck, as I frequently did, it's possible to pick up a few clues by reading a little of the solution. It might sound odd to point it out, but the way in which Smullyan explains the solutions tends to be remarkably readable, and that's an important part of the appeal of this book. Dare I say it, the solutions even begin to seem straightforward!

I'll give Smullyan's explanation in full, but first it's worth pointing out an important detail, which was not omitted by Smullyan, but was already covered in one of the introductory puz-

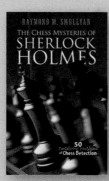

The Chess Mysteries of Sherlock Holmes
Raymond M. Smullyan
Dover Publications, 2012

zles. One of the consequences of the game being 'monochromatic' is that the knights are never able to move!

'The four missing knights were captured on their home squares. Then what pieces captured them? There is no problem at all accounting for the

white knights nor the black knight from g8. The only problem is the black knight from b8. What white piece could have captured it? It could not be the queen from d1, as she travels only on white squares. It could not be the bishop from c1, since the pawns on b2 and d2 have not moved to let it out. It certainly could not be the bishop from f1, because that bishop travels on white squares. Therefore, if the knight on b8 was captured by a queen or bishop, it must have been captured by a *promoted* queen or bishop. If the knight was captured by a *pawn*, then the pawn must have promoted! Now, the knight was not captured by the white king, since it would have taken the king at least fourteen moves to get there and back. And of course, it was not captured by a knight, as knights can't move. The last possibility to consider is a rook. Why couldn't the black knight have been captured by the rook from a1? This is the loveliest part of the problem. The reason

is that the rooks – since they are confined each to one colour, can go only an *even* number of squares forward, backward or sideways. In particular, the rooks from a1 and h1 can never possibly be on the second, fourth sixth or *eighth* rows! Therefore, if the black knight was captured by a rook, then it was captured by a *promoted* rook. This exhausts all possibilities, and we see that each of them involves the promotion of a White pawn. Q.E.D.'

There is actually another collection of Smullyan's retro-analysis problems called *The Chess Mysteries of the Arabian Knights*, which I haven't seen. Naturally, this kind of thing will not be to everybody's taste, and even if you like the puzzles, they might appear rather trivial, in the sense of being unconnected with any deeper insight. If you like puzzles, but are looking for something deeper, I can recommend tracking down a copy of some of Smullyan's other books, such as *Lady or the Tiger*, *To Mock a Mockingbird and Other Logic Puzzles* or *Forever Undecided: A Puzzle Guide to Gödel's Incompleteness Theorems*. Those books have nothing to do with chess, but Smullyan uses his training as a logician to come up with some really fiendish puzzles, which also happen to illustrate some really surprising and deep logical ideas, which are anything but trivial. It takes real skill to recast abstract ideas into a form which is accessible and entertaining, as well as challenging.

Another example of remarkably clear explanation takes us from retrograde analysis to a very different form of retrospective activity. I'm referring to *Vishy Anand: World Chess Champion*, co-authored by Vishy Anand and John Nunn. This book, which in an earlier incarnation won a BCF Book of the Year Award, is now in its third edition, and the timing is obviously apt given the forthcoming Anand-Gelfand match set to be played in May. It is above all a games collection, rather

than an autobiography. (Anand wrote in the introduction to the Second Edition, 'I don't want to spend too much time on biographical details, because this is a book about my games, so I will be content with a brief sketch.')

Nunn explains the basis of the third edition: 'The games in the previous (2001) edition of this book were all annotated by Vishy Anand, with myself (JN) checking the annotations.

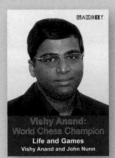

Vishy Anand: World Chess Champion
Vishy Anand and John Nunn
Gambit, 2012

This new edition adds 30 extra games, in which the roles are to some extent reversed. Vishy selected the games, which were then annotated by myself with the result going back to Vishy for checking.' An extra 30 games is a substantial addition to the earlier 57, and this latest edition also includes an interesting extended interview and biographical sketch written by Sean Marsh, so the whole thing runs to well over 500 pages. It might sound as though those last 30 games were simply 'tacked on', but that couldn't be farther from the truth. Nunn is one of very few writers capable of producing genuinely insightful annotations to someone else's games.

This book is full of wonderful games, many of which are tremendously complex, and occasionally the variations run to a considerable depth – neither Anand nor Nunn refrain from showing concrete variations, where the position warrants it. But both offer a nice balance of explanatory annotation as well, so there is a great deal of instructional value in here as well. Those explanations can come at some very concrete moments. I mentioned that I really

admired Smullyan's lucid solutions, and the following comment also made a great impression. [I have omitted a few additional variations.]

In a sharp game from the 1996 Amber Rapid, this position was reached, in which White to play would naturally be drawn to looking at the many different ways of giving discovered check. Nevertheless:

Anand-Polgar
Monte Carlo Amber Rapid 1996
position after 31...♖e2

31.bxc4!!

'I am very proud of this move, which was the main reason why I selected this game. Basically, I quickly rejected 31.♖g6+ followed by 32.♖xf6, because of 32...♗xf3+. Judit had gone much further in this line, but I couldn't be bothered – I wanted something cleaner. Black's pieces are perfectly placed; indeed the only piece which can be better placed is the e8-rook (aside from the black king, of course!). I noticed ♖g2+ followed by ♖xe2 and I also saw bxc4 in connection with the move c5, disturbing the black queen. Suddenly I realized that the d3-pawn could not move! Bingo!'
31...d2 32.♖g2+
1-0.

Perhaps there's something to be said for logic in chess after all!

P.S. The solution for the first diagram: The white king should be on c3. There was a black pawn on b4, a white pawn on c2 and the white king was on b3 when 1.c4 bxc3+e.p. 2.♔xc3+ followed. ∎

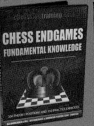

Jan Timman

Baden-Baden take decisive lead in Bundesliga

In the 1980s and early 1990s, two teams ruled supreme in the highest league of the German Bundesliga: Porz and Solingen. The battle for hegemony was fought out between two little towns around Cologne. Both teams were sponsored by millionaires. Egon Evertz paid the Solingen players, while Wilfried Hilgert financed those of Porz. The millionaires had garnered their riches in very different ways. Hilgert had become the richest man of Nordrhein-Westfalen through the herring trade. Evertz had specialized in manufacturing mechanical constructions.

It was usually Porz that captured the national title. In 1996 I started playing for the club, basking in their fame for a few seasons. But it wasn't to last. In the new millennium, new professional sponsors presented themselves, and the Baden-Baden team became especially strong. Porz no longer played first fiddle.

In 2006, Hilgert took a rigorous decision by withdrawing his first team from the highest league, which in fact meant eliminating Porz's second team. The second team played in the first league, so now players from the first team took over the boards there. Hilgert's official motive was that he did not agree with the clubs of the premier league forming their own association. Hilgert adamantly refused to be part of such a thing, suspecting that the tax authorities would soon slap a hefty tax bill on the newly formed association.

Michael Adams Man of the Match in clash with Werder Bremen

I do not know whether this happened or not. But I had noticed that our Maecenas could hardly bear losing a match in the top league. By voluntarily stepping down one rung, he had solved this problem.

And so Porz, led by Van Wely and myself, have been playing in the first league for many a season now. With four Dutch and two Ukrainian grandmasters we had a mercenary army that, time and again, marched out on a pointless mission. We became champion every year, but the number two went up to the premier league.

'They don't see us as rivals,' Van Wely once confided in me. And it's true that many teams didn't even bother to field their strongest players against us.

Yet it's not always easy. In January, during the Tata Steel tournament, we usually find the going hard. This year, half our team was in Wijk aan Zee. With four substitutes, Porz narrowly lost against Wiesbaden, which had Alekseev, Khenkin and Palac as their first three boards. We still claimed first place, but Wiesbaden went to the top league.

In that league, contrary to ours, January is a free month. Immediately after the Tata Steel tournament, a duel took place in the match Mülheim-Nord-Emsdetten between two young stars who have both been struggling with their form recently.

RG 3.4 – C42
**Maxime Vachier-Lagrave
Anish Giri**
Bundesliga 2011/12 (8)

1.e4 e5 2.♘f3 ♘f6 3.♘xe5 d6 4.♘f3 ♘xe4 5.♘c3

5...♘f6 Remarkable. In Reggio Emilia, Giri had swapped on c3 against Nakamura and went on to win in great style (for this game, with his commentary, see New In Chess 2012/1). But he must have been unsure about the opening, because in Wijk aan Zee he deviated against Topalov and went for a set-up in which both players are aiming to castle queenside. And now he deviates even earlier. The text-move à la Petrosian is fairly solid. White can only get an advantage by aiming to castle queenside. But Vachier-Lagrave chooses a quiet approach. **6.d4 ♗e7 7.h3 0-0 8.♗d3 ♖e8 9.0-0 b6 10.♖e1 ♗b7 11.♗f4 a6 12.♘e4 ♘bd7 13.♘fd2 ♘d5 14.♗h2**

14...f5

Sharp and ambitious, in vintage Giri style. He is challenging White to sacrifice a piece on f5.

With 14...♘b4 15.♗f1 ♘f6 he could have equalized fairly easily.

15.♘g3 g6 16.♕f3

Preparing the piece sacrifice on f5.

16...b5

17.♘xf5! There we are! The play will get very sharp now.

17...gxf5 18.♗xf5 ♘f8

A logical defence, but not the best move. It was important to involve the rook in the defence with 18...♖f8, after which the position is dynamically balanced. After the text White will be able to launch a strong attack.

19.c4 bxc4 20.♘xc4 c6

21.♗xd6

And White wins a third pawn for the piece, while keeping his positional advantage.

But he had an even stronger move. With 21.♖e4! he could have aimed for doubling rooks on the e-file, when Black would be in trouble, as witness 21...♔h8 22.♖ae1 ♘f6 23.♖4e3 ♘d5, and now 24.♗xd6! has gained in strength.

21...♗xd6 22.♖xe8 ♕xe8 23. ♘xd6 ♕e7 24.♕g3+ ♔h8 25.♖d1

White wants to involve his queen's rook in the attack as well.

25...a5 26.♖d3 ♗a6 27.♖f3

Intending 27...♗e2 28.♗xh7!.

27...♕g7

28.♕h4

With 28.♗g4! White could have preserved his advantage. After the text Black will just manage to hold on.

28...♕f6 29.♕xf6+ ♘xf6 30.♘f7+ ♔g7 31.♘e5 ♖a7 32.♘xc6 ♗b7 33.♖a3 ♖xb2 34.♖g3+ ♔f7 35. ♖a3 ♖b6 36.♘e5+ ♔e7 37.♖xa5 ♘e6 38.♘f3 ♔d6 39.♗xe6 ♔xe6 40.♖e5+ ♔d7 41.♖f5 ♔e7 42. ♖e5+ ♔d7 43.♖f5 ♔e7

Draw.

In the same way that the fight for the national title used to be fought out between Porz and Solingen, the two teams that usually battle it out now are Baden-Baden and Werder Bremen. Both teams have an impressive line-up of grandmasters. On paper, Baden-Baden is a shade stronger with Anand, Svidler and Adams – the World Champion and the champions of Russia and England on the first three boards. Bremen has Eljanov, Efimenko and Fressinet. A cautious conclusion would be that Baden-Baden has a bigger budget to spend. But for the competition itself it doesn't make all that much difference. What counts in the Bundesliga is match points. Both teams are strong enough to beat all other teams. Yet they both struggled in the beginning and both dropped points. In the second round, Baden-Baden slipped up against Mülheim, while Werder Bremen lost to Berlin a round later. Then they came back on track, with only Werder Bremen drawing with Eppingen, a lost match point that they would have to retrieve in their head-to-head.

In Round 12, halfway March, the clash of giants took place in Bremen. The usual approach in such matches is for players at a number of boards to opt for cautious manoeuvring, as they are acutely aware of the pressure. Strikingly enough, all Werder Bremen's white games bogged down in bloodless draws. But this didn't mean that Baden-Baden was better. After three hours all battles had been fought except for three boards. Theoretically interesting was the game on Board 7.

GI 7.15 – D93
Peter Heine Nielsen
Tomy Nybäck
Bundesliga 2011/12 (12)

1.♘f3 ♘f6 2.c4 g6 3.d4 ♗g7 4. ♘c3 d5 5.♗f4 0-0 6.e3 c5 7.dxc5 ♕a5 8.♖c1 dxc4 9.♗xc4 ♕xc5 10.♗b3 ♘c6 11.0-0 ♕a5 12.h3 ♗f5 13.♕e2 ♘e4 14.♘d5 e5

White's moves are also forced. Nielsen was still blitzing.

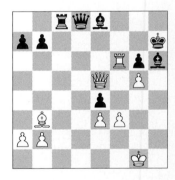

15.♗g5

A fairly unusual continuation, successfully used by Cmilyte recently. The move is based on an absolutely brilliant idea, which eventually turns out to be just insufficient for an advantage.

15...♘xg5

The principled reply. In practice, 15...♖ae8 has also been played, but I have the feeling that this might allow White to get an advantage.

16.♘xg5 ♕d8 17.h4

The start of a dangerous offensive that had also occurred in two games Cmilyte-Lahno. Nielsen knew these games, Nybäck did not.

17...h6

18.g4

The consequence of the previous move. There is no way back.

18...♗d7 19.♘e4 ♕xh4 20.f3

The subtle point of White's play is slowly emerging. White is going to take his rook to the h-file via f2.

20...♔h8

The only counterplay. Black is going to prepare pushing his f-pawn.

21.♖f2 f5 22.♖h2 ♕d8

23.♖xh6+! A beautiful rook sacrifice that Cmilyte herself also played.

23...♗xh6 24.♕h2 ♔g7

25.♖xc6! Everything is beautiful, but it's not enough for the win.

25...fxe4

Nybäck used up oceans of time, but always managed to find the only defence. In the first game Lahno played the spectacular 25...♗f4 here, but after the simple reply 26.♘xf4 White was winning. In the second game, one month later, Lahno opted for 25...♗xc6. The game was eventually drawn. Probably Heine Nielsen had found an improvement here.

26.♕xe5+ ♔h7

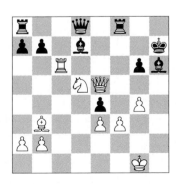

27.♘f6+ ♖xf6 28.♖xf6

28...♗e8!

Another important defensive move. Here, Nielsen thought for no fewer than 80 minutes. Meanwhile, Svidler, who had just drawn his game, had also studied the position. He didn't like what he saw at all. White will have to play very accurately to preserve the balance.

29.g5 ♖c8

The most logical continuation, although 29...♗xg5 and 29...♕d2 would also have been enough for equality.

30.♗d5?

This happens sometimes when a player thinks for too long. White makes a serious error. With 30.fxe4 he could have maintained the balance.

30...♗xg5

Nybäck had only seven minutes left for the remainder of his moves, otherwise he would undoubtedly have found the winning 30...♖c1+ 31.♔g2 ♕c8!, when the black queen threatens to penetrate with devastating force, leaving White nothing better than 32.♕xe4. Then Black can liquidate to a winning endgame with 32...♕c2+. After the text the position is balanced again.

31.♕xg5 ♔g7 32.♖f5 exf3 33.♕g3 ♕e7 34.♖xf3 ♖c1+ 35. ♖f1 ♖xf1+ 36.♔xf1 ♕f6+ 37.♔g1 ♕xb2 38.♕c7+ ♔h6 39.♕f4+ ♔g7 40.♕c7+ ♔h6

Draw.

A narrow escape for Baden-Baden. But the problems weren't over yet. Anand would also get into very hot water, and that game, too, was theoretically interesting.

SL 3.4 – D16
Vishy Anand
Pavel Eljanov
Bundesliga 2011/12 (12)

1.d4 d5 2.c4 c6 3.♘f3 ♘f6 4.♘c3 dxc4 5.a4 e6

In his comments to Game 19 of his 1935 match against Euwe, Alekhine observes about this move in the match book: 'Taking on c4 on the previous move is only effective in combination with developing the bishop to f5.'

An old-fashioned viewpoint, but he may well be right.

6.e4

This advance was first played by Alekhine in his first match game against Bogoljubow from 1929.

6...♗b4 7.e5

7...♘d5

Bogoljubow also played this. Euwe went 7...♘e4, but that move has passed out of use.

8.♗d2 b5 9.axb5 ♗xc3 10.bxc3 cxb5 11.♘g5

11...h6

Unusual. Black almost exclusively plays 11...♘c6 here. Anand probably intended to meet this with 12.h4, aim-

ing to develop the king's rook to h3. White has scored some good results with this plan recently.

12.♕h5 g6

Also interesting is the cool 12...0-0, as in Matlakov-Bologan, Plovdiv 2012. Black castles against the storm. After 13.♘e4 ♘c6 14.h4 f5 15.♘d6 ♗d7 White could have forced a draw with 16.♖h3. But he went 15.♖h3 and went on to win after a sharp battle.

13.♕h3 f5

A very compromising advance. On *ChessVibes* it is reported that Eljanov had forgotten his home analysis. That seemed strange to me. The position is dangerous for Black and each move is extremely important. This is not a time to indulge in forgetfulness.

14.exf6 e5

The intention of the previous move, but it does nothing to solve Black's problems.

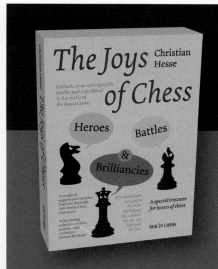

Jan Timman

15.f7+

Again Anand shows that he has problems finding his form. Very strong was 15.g4!, preparing to fianchetto his king's bishop. After 15...♗b7 16.♗g2 ♕xf6 17.♘e4 ♕e7 18.dxe5 ♕xe5 19.0-0 White has a large advantage. This line wasn't at all difficult to calculate. After the text an endgame eventually arises in which Black has nothing to complain about.

15...♔f8 16.♘e6+

16...♔e7! Is it possible that Anand had underestimated this king move?
17.♘xd8 ♗xh3 18.gxh3 ♖xd8 19. dxe5 ♔xf7 20.♗g2 ♘c6

21.0-0 White sheds the e-pawn to guarantee the open character of the game.

21...♘xe5 22.f4 ♘d3

Black cannot really prevent the f-file from being opened. 22...g5 is met very strongly by 23.♖a6!, with pressure play.
23.f5 gxf5 24.♖xf5+ ♔e6 25.♖h5 a5

Black has insufficient counterplay.
26.♖xh6+ ♔e5 27.♗e1 ♘5f4 28. ♗g3 ♔f5 29.♖f1 ♔g5 30.♖b6 ♖ab8 31.♖a6 ♖f8

Inaccurate. Good moves were 31...a4 and 31...♖a8.
32.h4+ ♔g4 33.♗f3+ ♔h3

34.♗d1

A tempting move. White wants to exploit the position of the black king. But it turns out to be impossible to go for mate.

Better was the simple 34.♖xa5, after which White keeps his endgame advantage.
34...♖g8 35.♖f3 ♖bd8 36.♔f1 ♘e5

Now the mate is gone and Black is getting the better chances.
37.♖xf4 ♖xd1+ 38.♔e2 ♖gd8 39.♖xa5 ♖1d2+ 40.♔e3 ♘g4+

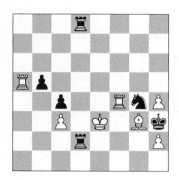

41.♔e4 It often happens that players blunder on move 40, with the time-control in sight. But even if they make the time-control, their concentration may flag. This is what happens here. White should have played 41.♔f3 and only play the king up the board after 41...♖d3+, the difference being that the black rook is less well positioned on d3 than on d2.

41...♖e8+

Eljanov fails to exploit White's lapse. With 41...b4! he could have created a very strong passed pawn. After 42.cxb4 c3 43.♖c5 c2 44.♖c3 ♖e2+ 45.♔f5 ♘e3+, followed by 46...♘d5, it is very doubtful whether White would have an effective defence.

42.♔f5

The situation is reasonably safe for White again.

42...♘e3+

With 42...♖d5+ Black could have kept some practical chances.

43.♔g6 ♘d5 44.♖xb5 ♘xf4+ 45. ♗xf4 ♖d3 46.h5 ♖xc3 47.h6 ♖b3 Draw.

After this second missed chance Werder Bremen's lot was virtually sealed.

After seven draws play only continued on Board 3, and here, Baden-Baden was firmly in control from the start.

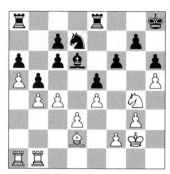

Adams-Fressinet
Baden-Baden-Werder Bremen
position after 29.c4

In a quiet line of the Ruy Lopez, White has built up a slight plus. This is the type of position in which Adams is at his best. He is in no danger of losing and can try to ratchet up the pressure.

29...c5

It would have been wiser to keep the position as closed as possible. If Black had swapped on c4, there would have been only one open file – a narrow base for White's winning chances. After the text White gets a passed a-pawn.

30.cxb5 axb5 31.bxc5 ♘xc5 32. ♖xb5 ♘xd3

33.♖a4 ♖a6 34.♖c4 c5 35.♘e3 ♖ea8 36.♖c3 ♘b4 37.♘c4 ♗e7 38.♖b3 ♘c6 39.♖b6 ♘b4 40.♔f3 ♖6a7 41.♗e3 ♔g8 42.♖b2 ♖c7 43.♔g4 ♔f7 44.♖b1 ♘c6 45. ♖1b5 ♘d4 46.♖b1 ♘c6 47.♖6b5 ♘d4 48.♖b7

After a lot of manoeuvring White is finally in the position to offer a rook swap in favourable circumstances.
48...♖xb7 49.♖xb7

49...♔e6

An instructive error. Normally speaking, centralization is necessary in the endgame, but in this situation, the black king is very unsafe in the centre. Correct was 49...♔f8, with chances of a successful defence.

50.♗d2 ♖a6 51.♗c3 ♗f8 52.f4

Threatening the devastating 53.f5+. Black is lost.

52...exf4 53.gxf4 f5+ 54.exf5+ ♔d5 55.♘e5 ♘e2 56.♗e1 ♗d6 57.♖xg7 ♗xf4 58.♘f7 ♘d3 59. ♘xd6 ♘xe1 60.♘e8 ♖xa5 61. ♖d7+ ♔c6 62.♖d6+ ♔b5 63.f6 ♖a7 64.♖e6 ♘d3 65.f7 ♖a4+ 66.♔g3

Black resigned.

This gave Baden-Baden a narrow victory, while a tie would have sufficed as well. With a lead of 3 match points and only two rounds to go it was safe to say that the championship was in the bag. ∎

JOHN SAUNDERS

Gawain Jones

CURRENT ELO: 2635

DATE OF BIRTH: 11 December 1987

PLACE OF BIRTH: Keighley, UK

PLACE OF RESIDENCE: London, UK

What is your favourite colour?
Green. When I was little I was in love with all things Robin Hood!

What kind of food makes you happy?
When I was living abroad I always craved Cornish pasties.

And what drink?
Pepsi Max and a nice (not warm!) beer after a long game.

Who is your favourite author?
It probably has to be Terry Pratchett. I like the books I read and TV I watch to make me laugh.

What was the best or most interesting book you ever read?
I found the books of Malcolm Gladwell's, such as *Outliers*, very interesting.

What is your all-time favourite movie?
I generally prefer TV series but I enjoyed *Shaun of the Dead* and *Hot Fuzz*.

What is your favourite TV series?
The BBC series *Sherlock*, although they are really more like films. They blend comedy and suspense.

Do you have a favourite actor?
Morgan and Martin Freeman. Very different people if you google them.

And a favourite actress?
My girlfriend would say the type of movies I watch don't have actresses in them.

What music do you like to listen to?
Old Pop-Rock stuff and silly humorous songs by people like Tim Minchin, Flight of the Conchords.

What was your best result ever?
The recent European Individual where I got 7½/11 and a 2760 performance.

What was the best game you ever played?
The one I was proud of for a long time was my win against Klaus Bischoff in 2006. It helped me on the way to my first GM norm. It was a Greek gift bishop sack too!

Who is your favourite chess player of all time?
While admiring the style of Tal and Morozevich, my favourite player has to be Kasparov.

Is there a chess book that had a profound influence on you?
I didn't know anything about chess history until I read Garry Kasparov's *My Great Predecessors* series.

What are chess players particularly good at?
We're all generally very competitive and so good at games and puzzles.

Do chess players have typical shortcomings?
I know I have a lousy sense of direction and a few other players I've spoken to have been the same. Then of course there are the social skills... Chess can be an all-consuming addiction and many people struggle to let go.

Do you have any superstitions concerning chess?
Not really although if I lose a game I tend to change my pen while if things are going well I try and keep in the same pattern.

What is the best chess country in the world?
Russia of course still has many of the top guys in the world, but other nations are catching up fast. It's scary all the Norwegian juniors coming up in Magnus' footsteps. Unfortunately it isn't any of the countries I've lived in. England lacks many serious tournaments but it's nice to see London confirmed this year. My girlfriend was very impressed when we found a copy of New In Chess in a shop in Germany, unheard of in either England or New Zealand.

Who or what would you like to be if you weren't yourself?
Ever since finding out it was possible to be a chess professional that's what I've wanted to be, so pretty happy being myself ☺.

Which three people would you like to invite for dinner?
Stephen Fry, Terry Pratchett and Plato!

Is there something you'd love to learn?
I speak some Italian, but I would love to be fluent in other languages.

What is your greatest fear?
I hate roller-coasters.

What would you save from your house if it were on fire?
Just my partner and me. The rest is replaceable.

What is the best thing that was ever said about chess?
'A good player is always lucky.'